UNLIKEABLE

UNLIKEABLE
THE PROBLEM WITH HILLARY

EDWARD KLEIN

REGNERY
PUBLISHING
A Division of Salem Media Group

Regnery® is a registered trademark of Salem Communications Holding Corporation

Cataloging-in-Publication data on file with the Library of Congress

ISBN 978-1-62157-378-4

Published in the United States by
Regnery Publishing
A Division of Salem Media Group
300 New Jersey Ave NW
Washington, DC 20001
www.Regnery.com

Manufactured in the United States of America

10 9 8 7 6 5 4 3 2 1

Books are available in quantity for promotional or premium use. For information on discounts and terms, please visit our website: www.Regnery.com.

Distributed to the trade by
Perseus Distribution
250 West 57th Street
New York, NY 10107

ALSO BY EDWARD KLEIN

NONFICTION

All Too Human:
The Love Story of Jack and Jackie Kennedy

Just Jackie:
Her Private Years

The Kennedy Curse:
Why Tragedy Has Haunted America's First Family for 150 Years

Farewell, Jackie: A Portrait of Her Final Days

The Truth about Hillary:
What She Knew, When She Knew It,
and How Far She'll Go to Become President

Katie:
The Real Story

Ted Kennedy:
The Dream That Never Died

The Amateur:
Barack Obama in the White House

Blood Feud:
The Clintons vs. the Obamas

NOVELS

If Israel Lost the War
(With Robert Littell and Richard Z. Chesnoff)

The Parachutists

The Obama Identity
(With John LeBoutillier)

ANTHOLOGIES

About Men
(With Don Erickson)

In memory of Richard Chesnoff, dear friend,
and Robert Christopher, mentor

CONTENTS

PROLOGUE "CALL OFF YOUR DOGS"   xi

PART I: A HELL OF A MESS

CHAPTER 1 "MORE GOLDA THAN MAGGIE"   3

CHAPTER 2 #GRANDMOTHERSKNOWBEST   7

CHAPTER 3 THE KING OF LITTLE ROCK   11

CHAPTER 4 INTIMATIONS OF MORTALITY   23

PART II: THE GREAT PRETENDER

CHAPTER 5 THE MISANTHROPE   37

CHAPTER 6 "I'VE ALWAYS BEEN A YANKEES FAN"   45

CHAPTER 7 A NEAR-DEATH EXPERIENCE   51

PART III: A PANTSUIT-WEARING GLOBETROTTER

CHAPTER 8 THE PRAETORIAN GUARD   65

CHAPTER 9 SHAFTED   71

CHAPTER 10 DOUBLE DIPPING   77

CHAPTER 11 "I LOVE YOU, BILLY"   81

CHAPTER 12 TOP TEN   85

PART IV: THE FLOODGATES OPEN

CHAPTER 13 "GET CAUGHT TRYING"   91

CHAPTER 14 IMAGINING "HILLARY 5.0"   101

CHAPTER 15 WOULDA, COULDA, SHOULDA   107

CHAPTER 16 "SKIN IN THE GAME"   119

CHAPTER 17 A "CLASSIC WASHINGTON OMELETTE"   133

CHAPTER 18 THE SMOLDERING GUN?   139

PART V: PICKING UP THE PIECES

CHAPTER 19 THE POLITICAL ANIMAL   147

CHAPTER 20 "WHEN YOU GOT IT, FLAUNT IT"   155

CHAPTER 21 DINNER WITH LIZ   159

PART VI: THE VENDETTA

CHAPTER 22 WHISPERING CAMPAIGN   167

CHAPTER 23 ON THE QT   177

CHAPTER 24 SOMEBODY "O'MALLEABLE"   181

CHAPTER 25 A SUB ROSA INVESTIGATION   187

CHAPTER 26 MISSING IN ACTION   191

CHAPTER 27 A TABLOID STAPLE   195

PART VII: SHAMELESS

CHAPTER 28 THE POTEMKIN CAMPAIGN   205

CHAPTER 29 ON THE "PRECARIOUS LEFT EDGE"   211

CHAPTER 30 "A HYDRA-HEADED BEAST"   217

CHAPTER 31 "IT'S GONE WAY TOO FAR"   223

EPILOGUE THAT OLD CAR SMELL   227

AUTHOR'S NOTE   239

NOTES   243

SELECTED BIBLIOGRAPHY   273

INDEX   277

"CALL OFF YOUR DOGS"

I've worked for four presidents and watched two others up close, and I know that there's no such thing as a routine day in the Oval Office.
—**Former vice president Dick Cheney**

Hillary sent word to the White House that she wanted to speak with Barack Obama.

Alone.

Just the two of them in the Oval Office. Without the intrusion of Valerie Jarrett, the president's consigliere and chief political strategist, or Michelle Obama, who frequently meddled in such Oval Office meetings.

Hillary didn't like or trust Jarrett and Michelle, and she knew that the feeling was mutual.

And so Hillary stipulated that she be allowed to see the president *privately*.

According to people who spoke directly with Hillary about the proposed meeting, she believed that Jarrett was behind the recent spate of damaging press leaks about foreign donations to the Clinton Foundation, Hillary's use of a private e-mail account, and her back-channel e-mail exchanges with Sidney Blumenthal.

When she discussed the matter with Bill Clinton, he opposed the meeting with Obama. He told her that it would accomplish nothing, and that Obama couldn't intervene to help her even if he wanted to, and he clearly didn't want to.

"He has a visceral dislike of me, and only a slightly less dislike of you," Bill said, according to sources close to Hillary who were interviewed for this book.

The Clintons then had one of their usual knock-down, drag-out shouting matches, and, as so often had happened in the past, when it was over Hillary chose to ignore Bill's advice.

She waited anxiously for word about the meeting from the White House.

—

According to an entirely different set of sources—in this case, people who spoke directly to Valerie Jarrett—Obama dreaded the prospect of being alone with Hillary.

Obama had had it with Hillary, these sources said. As far as he was concerned, Hillary had ignored his explicit warnings about her use of a private e-mail account, had breached a written agreement regarding foreign donations to the foundation, and had allowed the detested Blumenthal to poke his nose into State Department business.

Insulted and outraged, Obama had given Jarrett the green light to leak stories to the press about Hillary's crimes and misdemeanors. And Jarrett had gladly embraced her role as leaker in chief. Her explicit intention was to sabotage Hillary's chances of winning the Democratic Party's presidential nomination.

Obama had no doubt that Hillary wanted to confront him about these matters. He told Jarrett and Michelle that he was tired of listening to Hillary vent. The White House had allowed that to happen far too many times over the past several months. He didn't want to put himself through that ordeal again.

His answer to Hillary's request was a flat *No*.

There would be no meeting.

———

Eventually, however, Jarrett persuaded Obama to grant Hillary an audience.

"One way or another, you can't dodge her and you can't stall," she told him, according to the sources. "And there's nothing she can say that will change anything."

And so, bitterly and reluctantly, Obama agreed to meet with Hillary.

But only on one condition.

He wanted Jarrett with him in the Oval Office as a buffer when Hillary arrived.

—

Unlike most people who were about to meet with the president of the United States, Hillary wasn't the least bit intimidated by the aura of the man or his office. She had lived in the White House for eight years, had been in the Oval Office hundreds of times, was married to a president, and knew that he put his pants on one leg at a time just like every other man.

Jarrett, on the other hand, was used to people who acted obsequiously when they arrived to meet with the president, and she found Hillary's attitude to be imperious and condescending. In a bit of gamesmanship, she purposely kept Hillary waiting for more than a half hour.

"At first, Hillary pretended not to care that she was kept waiting," said a source who later spoke to Jarrett. "But when Hillary was ushered into the Oval Office, she was shocked to find Valerie standing next to the president, who was sitting behind his big oak desk."

"What can I do for you, Hillary?" Obama said.

He did not get up to greet her.

Hillary tried a friendly approach. She asked Obama for his advice on how to handle her troubles.

She didn't think she had done anything wrong, she said. She was being persecuted for minor, meaningless violations.

Obama acted as though he didn't know what she was talking about.

"He was almost being deliberately dense," said a Clinton source who spoke with Hillary shortly after the meeting and was later interviewed for this book. "It really angered her."

Everyone, including the president, knew that Hillary had a self-righteous side and a ferocious temper. She told friends that her father had been volcanic and that she, unfortunately, had inherited the trait.

Now, she lost the struggle to contain her composure.

"What I want for you to do is call off your fucking dogs, Barack!" she said, according to both Clinton and Jarrett sources, who independently confirmed the wording of Hillary's outburst.

Hillary later said that she regretted blowing up—not because she had been disrespectful to the president, but because she had revealed how much the charges against her had upset her. She let her antagonists see her vulnerability.

For a brief moment, Obama looked stunned. Then he stood up, turned his back on Hillary, and stared out the tall windows overlooking the Wilson Rose Garden.

Jarrett later said that she was afraid the president had been rendered speechless, something that rarely happened in all the years she had known him.

But before Jarrett could intercede, Obama spun around and looked directly at Hillary.

"There is nothing I can do one way or the other," he said. "Things have been set in motion, and I can't and won't interfere.

Your problems are, frankly, of your own making. If you had been honest...."

Hillary interrupted him.

"There are always haters out to get the Clintons," she said.

Later, Hillary told friends that she should have listened to Bill and not gone to the meeting. Now, however, all she wanted to do was get out of the Oval Office as quickly as possible.

She stood up, waved good-bye, and murmured "thank you" as she walked out, leaving the door of the Oval Office open behind her.

PART I

Cut to now, holy wow
When did everything become such a hell of a mess?
Maybe now, maybe now, can somebody come and take
this off my chest?
—Pink, "Are We All We Are"

CHAPTER 1

"MORE GOLDA THAN MAGGIE"

[Hillary is] about as likeable as elective surgery.
Every time she speaks, an angel shoots a cherub.
—**Greg Gutfeld, cohost of** Fox News' **The Five**

Hillary was taking lessons on how to be more likeable.

She was doing it for Bill, not for herself.

It was all his idea.

One evening while they were having drinks with friends, he turned to Hillary and said, "Let's ask Steven for help."

Their old Hollywood buddy Steven Spielberg could supply Hillary with acting coaches to help her when she had to give a speech.

Hillary didn't think she needed help.

"I get $250,000 to give a speech," she said, according to one of her friends, "and these Hollywood jackasses are going to tell *me* how to do it!"

But Bill insisted.

"Your policies and talking points are solid," he told her. "You can use Charlotte [Chelsea's baby daughter] to emphasize how you're all about women and children. Now the challenge is to repackage you in 2016 as a strong but loveable older woman—more Golda than Maggie."

Hillary didn't see the resemblance to Golda Meir or Margaret Thatcher, and she said, "I'm not going to pretend to be somebody I'm not."

But she carried on with the likeability lessons anyway.

Partly to please Bill.

But mostly to shut him up.

She hired an assistant to run a video camera in the den of Whitehaven, her home in the fashionable Observatory Circle neighborhood of Northwest Washington, D.C. It was just the two of them, her and the camera guy, who had to sign a confidentiality agreement so he couldn't blab to the press.

Later, after the recording session was over, she watched herself on the TV set. She sat in the dark, dressed in a blue muumuu that she'd recently purchased online at Amazon.com, and scrutinized her facial expressions, her hand gestures, the pitch of her voice, and her use of eye contact.

She told Bill she found the process tedious.

He said, "This could mean votes. Voters make decisions, even unconsciously, on how likeable a politician looks."

But it wasn't only the tedium that bothered her. She didn't like the results she saw from the Whitehaven video sessions.

For comparison, she screened videos that had been recorded live by her people when she was on the road and gave one of her six-figure speeches.* From the collection of videos, she selected the ones she liked and sent them off to Steven Spielberg's office, with a reminder that everyone involved in the project was sworn to secrecy.

Not that she had any reason to mistrust Steven. He'd always been more than generous to her. Spielberg let her use his corporate apartment in the Trump Tower on Manhattan's Fifth Avenue when she ran for a Senate seat from New York in 2000. Hillary felt right at home in the lavish surroundings, and she crashed at Spielberg's pied-à-terre more than twenty times. Accustomed as she was to being treated like royalty, she asked the management of Trump Tower to give her the exclusive use of one of its elevators. The management refused. She had to share an elevator with the skyscraper's other millionaire peons.

———

When the Hollywood coaches sent back their critiques of Hillary's video sessions, they noted that she looked irritated and bored.

Most times, after she glanced at the printout of their notes— she called them "notes from La-La Land"—she tossed them in the wastepaper basket.

---

* When the University of California at Los Angeles inquired whether Hillary would consider reducing her $300,000 fee, the answer came back from one of her aides: $300,000 *is* "the special university rate."

There was one thing about the process that she thought was worthwhile: working on her facial expressions.

If she got the facial expressions right, she believed the rest would fall into place. But as she pointed out to friends, she could just as easily work on her facial expressions in front of the bathroom mirror without having some Hollywood schmuck tell her what she was doing right or wrong.

"Sometimes they're helpful," she told the friends, "but just as often they're full of shit."

The truth was, Hillary Clinton did not take kindly to criticism. Let alone constant criticism.

It made her defensive and angry.

Which was her default expression when she spoke in public.

Which was her problem to begin with.

CHAPTER 2

#GRANDMOTHERSKNOWBEST

Don't be humble...you're not that great.
—Golda Meir

A couple of weeks after Hillary began her likeability lessons, she invited several women friends to Whitehaven. It was a frigid day in the middle of January 2015. The clock was ticking down to the first caucuses of the presidential race—the snows of Iowa were just a year away—and yet here was Hillary greeting her friends at the door and looking like a woman who didn't have a care in the world.

Her friends attributed her mellow mood to her surroundings. Whitehaven always put Hillary in a positive frame of mind.

Hillary had lived off the government teat for twenty-two years, starting with the day she and Bill moved into the governor's mansion in Little Rock in 1979. But in recent years, the Clintons' circumstances had radically changed. Thanks to their unconscionable speaking fees, gargantuan book advances, and shameless sweetheart deals, the Clintons were worth well in excess of $150 million—certainly rich enough to own a place of their own.

And what a place Whitehaven was.

The 5,152-square-foot neo-Georgian brick mansion had six bedrooms, a spacious ballroom, a dining room that could seat thirty people, and a backyard that was big enough for a tented party of several hundred union honchos, Hollywood bigfeet, Silicon Valley entrepreneurs, Wall Street *machers*, and well-fixed gentry liberals.

Whitehaven's rooms were painted in Hillary's favorite color (daffodil yellow) and hung with her favorite art (Haitian and Vietnamese). The living room featured a painting of Hillary and Chelsea wearing traditional Vietnamese conical hats made from bamboo and dried leaves.

Upstairs, Hillary had set aside a suite of rooms for Chelsea, whose lacerating temper made her more her mother's daughter than her father's.

Hillary had put her stamp on Whitehaven.

She bought the $2.85 million mansion out of the $8 million she was paid by Simon & Schuster for her memoir *Living History*, and she thought of the place as hers and hers alone.

It was *her* home.

Not Bill's.

He was hardly ever there.

The *Game Change* authors, John Heilemann and Mark Halperin, called Whitehaven Hillary's "dream house."

The *Hill*'s White House correspondent, Amie Parnes, called it Hillary's "fortress of solitude."

———

Hillary's friends gathered in the den and snuggled into over-stuffed Rose Tarlow sofas. They inquired after Chelsea's daughter, Charlotte Clinton Mezvinsky, who was four months old at the time. Hillary produced photos that showed her beaming with pleasure at her tiny granddaughter.

There was the usual chorus of oohs and ahhs.

Hillary said she planned to take Charlotte with her on the campaign trail as soon as the baby was old enough to travel. Charlotte would help her play the loveable grandmother card and win over women voters. It apparently never occurred to Hillary that she would be exploiting her daughter and the child. The Barbara Lee Family Foundation, which did research on women running for public office, urged female candidates to use personal experiences to improve their likeability, and Hillary already had an unofficial hashtag to burnish her image: #GrandmothersKnowBest.

When one of her friends noticed a video camera standing on a tripod in a corner of the room, she asked Hillary what it was for.

"Speech practice," Hillary said, according to the recollection of one of the women. "My coaches tell me I'm supposed to *pretend* when I speak. Pretend that I actually like the audience. I'm supposed to force myself to keep a smile on my face. I'm supposed to think happy thoughts. To think of Chelsea or Charlotte or my

[late] mother. But not about Bill, because even though I love him to death, he makes me tear my hair out."

That got a laugh from the women.

Her friends often joked (though never to Hillary's face) that the characters of Frank and Claire Underwood in Netflix's Emmy Award–winning series *House of Cards* were a send-up of Bill and Hillary Clinton. Kevin Spacey, who plays the villainous Frank Underwood, might have been mouthing the Clintons' maxim when he said, "In politics, you either eat the baby or you are the baby."

Like the Underwoods, the Clintons were a perfectly matched pair: they were driven by vaulting ambition; they constantly schemed against their enemies, real and imagined; they were cold-blooded when it came to getting what they wanted; and according to one of Hillary's closest friends, they hadn't shared the same bed in years.

But unlike the fictional Frank and Claire, Bill and Hillary were hardly ever in the same place at the same time. They lived completely separate lives.

They spoke on the phone every day—sometimes a dozen or more times a day—but Hillary rarely knew where Bill was and what he was up to.

He didn't tell her and she didn't ask.

Because she didn't want to know.

CHAPTER 3

THE KING OF LITTLE ROCK

I don't care what you think unless it is about me.
—Kurt Cobain, "Drain You"

Even in failing health—gaunt, trembling, hobbled by progressive heart disease—Bill Clinton was an object in perpetual priapic motion.

When the fancy took him, he'd climb aboard a borrowed Gulfstream G650—a sumptuous $65 million twin-engine jet that seated sixteen, had a range of seven thousand nautical miles, cruised at fifty-one thousand feet, and flew nearly at the speed of sound—and take off for another round of pleasures and self-indulgences.

Today, he might be in Los Angeles—caught by paparazzi posing with two prostitutes from the Moonlite BunnyRanch brothel of Mound House, Nevada.

Tomorrow, he might be in Toronto—on his way to dinner with one of his rumored mistresses.

The next day, he might be in Lima, the capital of Peru—traveling with Scarlett Johansson.

Or in Lagos, Nigeria....

Or Port-au-Prince, Haiti....

He was like the Flying Dutchman, the captain of the legendary ghost ship that never made port.

The news media covered his appearances at the meetings of the Clinton Global Initiative. Reporters and TV cameras were on hand for his speeches and TV interviews. But they invariably lost track of him after that.

It was no use sending a reporter to stake out the Clinton homes in Chappaqua and Whitehaven; Bill rarely turned up at either place, and when he did, it was for a quick lunch or dinner, and then he was gone in a flash. He spent most of his downtime concealed from the national press corps in plain sight—in Little Rock, Arkansas.

He had everything a narcissist could possibly want in Little Rock: the Bill and Hillary Clinton National Airport; the William J. Clinton Presidential Center and Park; the University of Arkansas Clinton School of Public Service; a spacious penthouse apartment with smart TVs in every room and a golf-chipping lawn on the terrace; a catering service from his own four-star restaurant located in the basement of his presidential library; hot and cold running women; and a street named after him.

It was good to be king of Little Rock.

When his Secret Service Escalades trundled down President Clinton Avenue, adoring crowds stopped and waved at him. If he spotted some attractive women on the sidewalk, he got out and pressed the flesh, literally and figuratively. During the day, he went around dressed in a University of Arkansas Razorback T-shirt and SoulCycle shorts. At night, he threw parties atop the library. You could always tell when Bill was holding court from the bright glow that flickered from the windows of his penthouse like the tantalizing light at the end of Daisy Buchanan's dock in *The Great Gatsby.*

—

But even when Bill was tucked away in Little Rock, he kept Hillary in the dark about his whereabouts and activities.

That, of course, was nothing new.

Throughout their forty-year marriage, Bill's catch-me-if-you-can lifestyle raised questions about his allegiance to his wife. These questions went beyond his famous philandering. There were doubts about the sincerity of his commitment to Hillary's political career. Sometimes he acted as though he felt that his wife's elevation would diminish him.

He said or did impetuous, controversial things that seemed to come out of left field and that embarrassed Hillary and caused her serious political damage. The most famous example of his mischief making came during the 2008 presidential primary season when he angered black voters and turned them against

Hillary by denigrating Obama's victory in South Carolina by comparing it to Jesse Jackson's wins there in the 1980s.

But there were other examples of Bill's political infidelity.

When Hillary said at a press conference that some of the thirty thousand "personal" e-mails she deleted were between her and her husband, Bill let it be known through his spokesman that he had sent a grand total of two e-mails during his entire life. More recently, when Karl Rove suggested that Hillary suffered a serious health episode after fainting and suffering a concussion in 2012, Bill made matters worse by revealing that it took Hillary "six months of very serious work to get over" her injury. Hillary's health, Bill admitted, would be a "serious issue" in the 2016 campaign.

Sometimes, Hillary told friends, she suspected that Bill really didn't want her to become president.

That wasn't true.

But it wasn't far off the mark, either.

According to several of Bill's advisers who were interviewed for this book, he expressed mixed feelings about Hillary's presidential ambitions. He understood her desire to become a historic figure as the first woman president of the United States. And he intended to campaign for her hard; he would give it everything he had.

Yet, at the same time, he had major reservations about Hillary's running for president. As he saw it, her campaign—win or lose—posed a threat to the regal world he had established for himself since leaving the White House.

That world centered on the Clinton Foundation.

"The worst case scenario for the foundation, its allies say privately, would be if [Hillary] lost her presidential campaign in a manner similar to the way she lost her 2008 race to then-Sen. Barack Obama, which at least temporarily tarnished the family's political brand," reported *Politico*. "Unlike 2008, a losing 2016 campaign would effectively end the political ambitions of Bill or Hillary Clinton. That would thrust responsibility for the [Clinton Foundation's] future squarely into the hands of their daughter. While she is being groomed to take over the family's political dynasty, thus far she has not demonstrated her parents' fundraising prowess or leadership ability."

—

Ever since he left the White House under a cumulus of scandal, Bill had focused on one overriding goal: to rehabilitate his reputation. The Clinton Foundation and its glitzy conference offshoot, the Clinton Global Initiative, were the chosen instruments of his redemption. His good works with the foundation were designed to transform him from a president who had debased the dignity of his office into a living national treasure.

However, no sooner did Hillary announce on April 12, 2015, that she was running for president than the foundation came under withering criticism. And this time Bill and Hillary couldn't blame the Vast Right-Wing Conspiracy for their problem. Liberal organs like the *New York Times* and the *Washington Post* did deep dives into the foundation's pay-for-play activities. *Politico* quoted a former Clinton aide who called it "a media whack-fest."

The Clintons hadn't suffered such a battering since the Monica Lewinsky scandal. And they were clearly unprepared to handle it.

When NBC News' Cynthia McFadden asked Bill if he saw anything wrong with accepting $500,000 apiece for speeches while his wife was secretary of state, he came up with a ludicrous answer.

"I gotta pay our bills," said the man who was rated the wealthiest living ex-president, and who was among the top-ten wealthiest of all time.

He gave an equally ridiculous answer to a question about why the foundation had failed to include tens of millions of dollars in donations on its tax returns.

Everybody makes mistakes on their taxes.

His self-justifying response reminded everyone of Hillary's outlandish claim that she and her husband were "dead broke" upon leaving the White House.

——

Until the foundation scandal hit, Bill had been flying high in the opinion polls. An NBC/*Wall Street Journal* poll conducted in the spring of 2015 showed that 56 percent of people had a positive view of the former president. That was twelve points higher than either Barack Obama or Hillary Clinton. With the eruption of the Clinton Foundation scandal, however, Bill's stature as the most popular person in American politics was seriously threatened.

A Niagara of funny money flowed into the Clinton Foundation's coffers from dodgy foreign businessmen, despotic foreign governments, petrostates like Saudi Arabia and the United Arab Emirates, and homegrown special-interest groups that expected a quid for their quo—anti–free trade labor unions, anti-regulation hedge funds, too-big-to-fail Wall Street banks, global-warming billionaires, and American corporations with massive lobbying operations in Washington.

Millions more came from speaking fees earned by Bill, Hillary, and Chelsea Clinton, which they transferred to the foundation slyly, like con artists playing three-card monte. The Clintons failed to report these fees on financial disclosure forms even though government ethics rules clearly stated that "the source, date and amount of payments made or to be made directly to a charitable organization in lieu of honoraria must...be disclosed."

Like everything else that Bill and Hillary touched, the foundation was a sketchy operation that skirted legality and often fell over the edge. With its embarrassment of riches—it had collected $2 billion since its creation—it was able to do a smattering of good work, especially in the areas of healthcare, AIDS, and addressing poverty in Africa. But it spent money indiscriminately, and mostly on itself. According to the Federalist's Sean Davis, for every ten dollars that the foundation took in, it disbursed only one dollar to charitable causes. The other nine dollars went to euphemisms like "office supplies" and "travel."

"This data," wrote Jonathan S. Tobin in *Commentary* magazine, "is a reminder that the main point of the Bill, Hillary and Chelsea Foundation is to support its namesakes in a lavish fashion and allow wealthy donors access to them.... Most of the money spent by the foundation is geared toward providing access for the donors to the Clintons via the annual [Clinton Global Initiative] celebrity conference and events at the [Clinton] Library."

The foundation had a random way of selecting which causes it supported, but basically it came down to whatever Bill wanted. Money went to everything from sustainable farming in South America to saving elephants in Africa.

Often the foundation's goals seemed indistinguishable from those of the hard Left of the Democratic Party. The foundation supported such progressive causes as teachers unions, public service unions, "human-made global warming" education, higher taxes on the rich, and the redistribution of wealth.

The foundation had a huge field organization, which could be transformed with a snap of Bill's fingers into a get-out-the-vote army for Hillary's presidential campaign. Bill treated these foot soldiers with his customary grandiosity; from time to time, he sent out a memo encouraging them to take their spouses to an expensive dinner and charge the meal to the foundation.

Beyond the power and the money, Bill derived personal pleasure from being the top dog of the foundation. It was the means by which he conducted the most fun-filled post-presidency in American history.

But now, it appeared that Bill's days of wine and roses might be over. He was going to find it harder to solicit donations from his foreign friends—something he enjoyed doing and was very good at. And from now on, he'd have to look over his shoulder before he climbed aboard a G650 private jet with a posse of pretty things.

Life was going to get rough for the old reprobate.

Which made him all the more ambivalent about Hillary's presidential ambitions.

When it came to Bill Clinton's true intentions, it was hard to read the tea leaves.

For instance, during one of Bill's appearances on the *Late Show with David Letterman*, Dave asked the former president if he would move back into the White House if Hillary won the election in 2016.

"If she wins the election," Bill replied, "the chances are 100 percent I'll move back."

Then he added, "If—wait, wait—if I'm asked."

"You may not be invited back," Dave joked.

"My experience is that since I left the White House, when a president of either party asks, you say yes," Bill said. "So I hope I'll be invited."

But according to one of Bill's trusted legal advisers who was interviewed several times for this book, Bill's line of thought was not as simple as that.

"Bill told me that if Hillary is elected president, he wasn't going to give up his other interests and take up residency in the White House, the way first ladies have traditionally done," the adviser said. "He'll continue spending a good amount of time at his penthouse in Little Rock. He'll continue to travel on foundation business. And he'll spend time in Haiti, which is still a mess and something he very much wants to make right. He is worried about his legacy with Haiti.

"He is also going to travel to Africa on his AIDS initiatives," the adviser continued. "He'll personally visit pharmaceutical corporations to work on getting cheaper or free AIDS medications for the worst hit countries. He'll continue to make speeches. He's going to lecture at the University of Arkansas Clinton School of Public Service.

"It's a very ambitious schedule that doesn't include sitting around the White House. Of course, he'll be there often. He's going to have a sock drawer there. He'll attend state dinners when it seems appropriate. But he's planning to not hover around so that people aren't sure who is president. He's going to back off and let Hillary be president."

If Bill didn't intend to be a permanent resident in the White House in the event Hillary won the presidency, who would take on the traditional responsibilities of the first lady?

"There is a social function to the first lady's role, and that will not go away," said Susan Swain, coauthor of a history on first ladies. "It is important to have somebody in that role. The best guesstimate with the Clintons is that Chelsea Clinton would take over that role."

So which was it?

Would Bill move back into the White House?

Or stay away for long stretches of time?

Maybe Bill didn't know the answer himself. He often said things that he didn't mean but that suited his purpose when he said them. It didn't matter if he was caught in a contradiction or an outright lie. Like Hillary, he was shameless, a person without a moral center. He could pursue two opposing objectives at the same time without feeling a twinge of guilt. For instance, he could treat Barack Obama as his sworn enemy *and* deliver a rousing speech for Obama at the Democratic National Convention.

If Hillary became president, Bill might very well refuse to play the game of first gentleman, as his adviser said.

Or he might lay claim to Hillary's old office on the second floor of the West Wing and renew the Clintons' warped version of their contract with America: two for the price of one.

CHAPTER 4

INTIMATIONS OF MORTALITY

Sans teeth, sans eyes, sans taste, sans everything.
—**William Shakespeare,** As You Like It

Toward the end of April 2015, Bill and Hillary summoned their top advisers to a crisis meeting at Chappaqua.

It was time to scramble the jets.

When the long-awaited launch of Hillary's presidential campaign finally occurred, it was nearly scuttled by a tsunami of scandals: Benghazi…exorbitant speaking fees…deleted e-mails… dodgy foundation fund-raising…special business favors from the Obama administration and the Clinton Foundation for Hillary's brother.

Instead of getting a bounce from her road trip to Iowa and New Hampshire in her cutesy Scooby Doo van, Hillary was losing in some matchup polls with potential Republican challengers in critical swing states.

Several old Clinton hands made the trek to Chappaqua for the meeting, including John Podesta, Bill's former chief of staff, and James Carville and Paul Begala, the top strategists of Bill's 1992 presidential campaign. When they arrived at the Clintons' Dutch Colonial house on 15 Old House Lane, the garden was blooming with neat rows of pink tulips, and the swimming pool was uncovered after the long, bitter winter.

The Clintons were waiting for them in the den along with Huma Abedin, Hillary's alter ego; her chief of staff Cheryl Mills; and a smattering of close personal friends. The atmosphere, according to one of the participants who was interviewed for this book, resembled an Irish wake—a mix of gloom over Hillary's troubles and good-natured banter.

All three of the TV sets were tuned to the news from Baltimore, where rioters had torched buildings and cars and looted a CVS pharmacy. The phone was constantly ringing with updates from the scene of the violence. One of the calls came from Elijah Cummings, the African American representative from Maryland's Seventh Congressional District, who was in Baltimore observing the mayhem and reporting back to Bill.

Huma handed the phone to Bill. He was sipping red wine, which his cardiac specialist had told him was good for his heart condition.

As he listened, Bill smiled and gave Hillary the thumbs-up sign.

As he hung up the phone, he said, "That was good news from Elijah."

Bill explained that the rioting denizens of Baltimore had just given Martin O'Malley, one of Hillary's rivals for the nomination, a rough time. The former Maryland governor had cut short a trip to London and Dublin and returned to Baltimore, where he had once served as the city's mayor. But as he walked the streets, hoodie-wearing agitators heckled and booed him. The rioters blamed O'Malley for the aggressive zero-tolerance police tactics that, they charged, had led to the death of a black man named Freddie Gray and touched off the riots.

"Baltimore isn't local; it's the number one issue for the [party's] base right now," Bill said. "They care that their young men are the constant target of police violence. They don't care about Hillary's goddamn e-mails. If O'Malley comes after us, we've got to make sure we get that message out. He let the police get out of control. Encouraged the violence against African American youth. That's devastating for O'Malley."

Suddenly, an expression of pain crossed Bill's face, and he sat down on a sofa. He patted a pillow with the Seal of the President of the United States and tugged at the muscles in his neck, as though he were trying to ease the pain. Hillary came over and sat next to him. She took his hand and rubbed it.

In a moment, Bill seemed to recover. He began to talk about the upcoming presidential election.

"I'm not sure how much good I can do," he said. "I'm not mad enough. I don't hate the people that'll be in the race enough.

You have to have that hate to knock them out. I'm tired and weary."

—

Everyone knew that Bill Clinton was not a well man.

On the TV screen, he looked haggard and drained of energy. His complexion ranged from sallow to cadaverous. His cheeks were hollow. His shirt collar hung around his neck. His hands trembled. He had trouble getting words out. He was sixty-eight years old—by today's standards, still middle aged—but he looked and acted like an old man.

When he wasn't performing for the public—when he let down his guard in private—he looked and acted even worse.

He took long naps. He chose to sit rather than stand, to ride rather than walk, to nibble rather than eat. He talked incessantly about his mortality, about what was in his last will and testament, about how he had been dealt a bad hand in his DNA. He had a history of heart disease on his mother's side of the family going back several generations, and his cholesterol level was through the roof.

Up until ten years or so ago, he had been in denial about his health. He ate and drank whatever he wanted, exercised only sporadically, and let himself go to seed. He was more than fifty pounds overweight.

In 2004, Doctor Allan Schwartz, a cardiologist at New York–Presbyterian/Columbia Medical Center, warned Bill that he was a walking time bomb; an angiogram revealed that he had arterial blockage of 90 percent in several places. He was a candidate for a massive heart attack. It was only then that the former president faced up to reality and agreed to undergo quadruple coronary artery bypass surgery.

He became a vegan (though he ate salmon and had an occasional omelet) and adopted a plant-heavy diet in the hope of reversing his heart disease.

Six months later, however, he was rushed to the hospital for another operation—this one to remove scar tissue and fluid from his left chest cavity. Then in 2010, after complaining of chest pains, he was taken by ambulance to New York–Presbyterian/ Columbia, where two coronary stents were implanted in the coronary arteries that carried oxygen to the heart.

In the late spring of 2013, Doctor Schwartz informed Bill that there was further deterioration in the function of his heart. His heart disease was progressive. There was little Bill could do about it except cut back on his hectic schedule and get more rest.

But shortly after being given that depressing prognosis, Bill heard that his friend, ninety-one-year-old Henry Kissinger, had undergone successful heart-valve replacement surgery at Massachusetts General Hospital. Bill flew to Boston to see Kissinger's doctor, the eminent cardiologist Timothy Edward Guiney.

Could Doctor Guiney save his life?

Guiney was not optimistic. During Bill's three emergency operations, parts of his heart muscle had died. At Bill's age, new heart blockage could occur at any time and it might prove fatal.

It was an open question whether he could stand the rigors of Hillary's presidential campaign.

That summer after Bill saw Doctor Guiney, he and Hillary rented a home in Sagaponack, a resort village on the East End of Long Island. The $11 million house sat on three and a half acres and rented for $200,000. The Clintons took along their three dogs—Seamus, an old chocolate lab; Tally, a poodle; and a stray puppy named Maisie.

Bill liked to sit by the pool, sip a fresh vegetable drink, and let his legs dangle in the heated water while he schmoozed with friends.

"Everybody thinks I'm about to die," he said one day. "They're already trying to bury me. But I'm not going anywhere until we get back in the White House. That's going to happen. It's true that the news from the doctors hasn't been all that good. But I'm going to stick around and surprise everybody."

——

Hillary was naturally worried about Bill. But she was also concerned about her own mounting health issues.

Blinding headaches frequently plagued her, and she constantly worried that she was developing another blood clot on her brain. There were incidents on the campaign trail when she felt faint and nearly swooned. Those incidents were kept secret.

The last time she fainted, in 2012, she was rushed to the hospital, where doctors told her that she had a right transverse venous thrombosis, or blood clot, between her brain and skull.

Her doctors informed Hillary that she had an intrinsic tendency to form blood clots, and that she had to take an anticoagulant and be carefully monitored for the rest of her life.

Another thing that concerned her was the trembling in her hands. This had been going on for some time, but the condition seemed to be getting worse. She consulted a neurologist, who told her it was nothing to be overly concerned about, but to keep an eye on it and have periodic checkups.

"She's been a strong soldier through many political campaigns, but the trembling in her hands really concerns her," her friend said. "For the first time since I've known her, she's showing self-doubt about her strength and vitality.

"The recent stuff in the papers about her brother Tony's dodgy financial deals really got to her," the friend went on. "She says that all presidents and their wives have crazy brothers who embarrass them, and that she's no exception. But Hillary's never had any control over Tony. He's been a repo man and taken other questionable moneymaking jobs. Tony's definitely one of the things that keeps Hillary awake at night."

Hillary was having trouble sleeping. She woke up frequently and found it hard to get back to sleep. Her insomnia worried her because it sapped her energy just when she needed it the most for the campaign.

"She is exhausted and depressed a lot of the time," one of her friends said. "She has been offered Ambien and Lunesta by her doctors. She had taken those medications in the past, but she said they made her less sharp the next day."

—

In an effort to divert attention from Hillary's escalating e-mail scandal, her campaign released a report in late July 2015 on her medical condition from her personal physician, Doctor Lisa Bardack. According to Doctor Bardack, tests revealed "a complete resolution of the effects of the concussion as well as total dissolution of the thrombosis."

But that was not the whole story. In fact, Hillary's uncertain health had forced her to cancel several meetings and cut back on her campaign schedule. She swore to friends that her doctors couldn't find any definitive problem, but Bill believed she was in denial and was ignoring what could be life-threatening symptoms.

Bill was so concerned that he asked a well-known cardiologist to review Hillary's medical records. After looking over her cardiograms and X-rays and other records, the cardiologist recommended that Hillary travel with a full-time physician who would keep her under constant observation.

"Most politicians are reluctant to be monitored by a doctor because they fear that if the results are leaked to the press, the information might harm their chances of election," the cardiologist said in an interview for this book. "But doctors are discreet. And in Hillary's case, it is very important that she be monitored on a daily basis. Her symptoms—the fainting—are very worrisome, especially for someone of her age. I have a lot of experience with political candidates and have seen the toll that the stress of a campaign can take. It's stressful for young candidates, and for older ones like Hillary, it's beyond belief."

Hillary admitted to one of her best friends that she often got "dizzy" and "woozy."

"But she told me that there was no need for a full-time doctor to travel with her on the campaign trail," this friend said in an interview. "Bill insisted any way, and he approached Dean Ornish [the founder of the nonprofit Preventive Medicine Research Institute in Sausalito, California] to help find a suitable doctor. Ornish has been close to the Clintons for twenty years. It was he who put Bill on a plant-based vegan diet. And he might become surgeon general if Hillary gets into the White House."

■

Bill's worst fear was that Hillary would stumble physically or fall at a critical moment in the campaign and reveal that she wasn't up to handling the job of commander in chief. One night in their bedroom at Chappaqua, he gently approached the question of how the presidential campaign was affecting her health.

"Bill told me that he tiptoed into the dangerous territory of suggesting that maybe Hillary should rethink whether she had the physical stamina to take on the tortures of a presidential campaign," said one of Bill's closest friends. "Hillary blew up and said, 'You're acting like a fucking quitter and a loser. You're projecting your own health problems onto me. I'm not dying.'

"Bill raised both hands in surrender and said, 'Don't shoot,'" the friend continued. "Hillary had a hairbrush in her hand, and Bill was afraid she was going to throw it at him. But she restrained herself with great effort.

"He wants her to be president, but he doesn't want her to kill herself doing it. He told me he has tried to bring up the subject with Chelsea, thinking that she would share his concern about her mother's health. But Chelsea has her mother's determination and passion to go on no matter what the cost. There is no way that Bill is going to get any help from her."

—

It was a short distance from the Chappaqua house to Bill's home office, which was located in a converted red barn. However, after the crisis meeting with Podesta, Carville, and Begala, Bill didn't feel well enough to make it to the barn on his own. He climbed into a golf cart and, with Hillary and her friends keeping pace beside him, scootered over to the barn. It was full of his favorite books and souvenirs from his travels, including an incongruous cigar-store Indian.

After a while, another old Clinton hand, Donna Shalala, made an appearance. A tiny, energetic woman with close-cropped hair, Shalala had served as the secretary of health and human services under President Clinton, and then transitioned into a career as president of the University of Miami. She was known as a tough, no-nonsense manager, and Hillary had asked her to take over as the Clinton Foundation's new president and chief executive. The previous president of the foundation had quit in disgust over its dubious practices.

"Donna was one of Hillary's closest friends and most trusted operators," said a source with knowledge of Shalala's appointment as head of the foundation. "They had served together on the board of the Children's Defense Fund. Hillary was sorry that Donna had stayed as long as she had at the University of Miami, because Hillary was convinced that the chaos at the foundation wouldn't have happened if Donna had been in charge.

"Hillary hoped that Donna would crack the whip and set things right again," the source continued. "She was convinced that the Obamas would like nothing better than to see the foundation go down in flames—and her reputation with it. Privately, among a few very close friends, Hillary admitted that things were even worse at the foundation than had been reported in the *Times* and elsewhere. It was a hell of a mess."

Bill was extremely fond of Donna, too, but he had opposed her appointment. He saw it as an unwanted intrusion into the affairs of his personal enterprise. He didn't make a distinction between himself and the foundation; they were one and the same to him. But Hillary had convinced him that the foundation had to be given a top-to-bottom scouring and that Donna would apply a stiff brush.

Bill didn't hold it against Donna that she had accepted the job. In fact, he couldn't hide his pleasure at seeing her, and he greeted her with a hug and kisses.

Donna was all business. She didn't waste time telling Bill and Hillary exactly what she intended to do as the new CEO of the foundation.

"I'm going to run the place as a *normal* foundation in terms of fund-raising and spending," she said.

Hillary nodded her head.

Bill snorted when Donna used the word "normal."

"His attention seemed to wander," one of the Clintons' friends recalled in an interview, "and in the middle of the discussion, he got up from his chair, walked across the room with his back to Donna, and patted his wooden cigar-store Indian on the head, as though it was a talisman. I got the distinct impression that, no matter what Donna said or did, Bill was going to do it his way."

PART II

THE GREAT PRETENDER

Oh yes, I'm the great pretender
Pretending that I'm doing well
My need is such, I pretend too much
I'm lonely, but no one can tell
—Buck Ram, "The Great Pretender"

CHAPTER 5

THE MISANTHROPE

Betrayed and wronged in everything,
I'll flee this bitter world where vice is king....
—*Moliere,* The Misanthrope

Bill Clinton's ambivalence about Hillary's political future must have sent chills down her spine, for as the feminist author Camille Paglia pointed out, Hillary had never found a way to succeed "without her husband's connections, advice, and intervention."

In fact, it was debatable whether anyone would have heard of Hillary Rodham if it hadn't been for William Jefferson Clinton.

Throughout her marriage, Bill had always been the leader, the brilliant and successful politician, and she had always been the follower and beneficiary of his power and influence:

- Hillary was asked to join Little Rock's prestigious Rose Law Firm in the 1970s *only after* Bill ascended to the post of Arkansas attorney general, the chief legal officer who dealt on a daily basis with the state's law firms.
- She was made a partner in the Rose Law Firm *only after* Bill was elected governor of the state, with all the patronage and influence that that office possessed.
- She was elected a U.S. senator thanks to the wave of sympathy *created by* Bill's dalliance with Monica Lewinsky, which lent Hillary a much-needed aura of vulnerability as the wronged woman. She also profited from the *votes Bill bought for her* by granting pardons to crooked New York Hassidim and violent Puerto Rican nationalists.
- She was appointed secretary of state *in large part because* Barack Obama desperately wanted to sideline Bill Clinton and thwart his plots and intrigues.
- Even now, her chief political asset was not herself; it was Bill. No one ever had to give Bill Clinton lessons in likeability.

———

If Hillary's career was defined by her connection to Bill Clinton, her character was shaped by her parents.

Her father, Hugh Rodham Sr., a former naval drill instructor, was abusive. As I wrote in *The Truth about Hillary*:

Some visitors to the Rodham home recalled Hugh Sr. as a scary figure—a barrel-chested man with a booming voice, who was always criticizing Hillary's posture and telling her: "Head up, chin in, chest out, stomach in!" An acquaintance once described him as "tougher than a corn cob, as gruff as could be."

"Among both relatives and friends," wrote Roger Morris in *Partners in Power*, "many thought Hugh Rodham's treatment of his daughter and sons amounted to the kind of psychological abuse that might have crushed some children."

In her memoir *Living History*, Hillary strongly suggested that her father was a sadist who humiliated her mother and beat her brothers.

The presence of a warm, loving mother might have assuaged the pain inflicted on Hillary by her father. But Hillary's mom, Dorothy Howell Rodham, was of little help in that regard.

Dorothy had been abandoned at the age of eight by her own mother and sent on a cross-country train ride with her three-year-old sister to Alhambra, California, where her grandparents lived. There, Dorothy was so cruelly abused by her grandparents that she ran away from home.

Scrappy and competitive, Dorothy believed that the world was a dog-eat-dog place. She taught Hillary that she had to *act* as though she were brave even when she *felt* sad or fearful.

"If Suzy hits you," Dorothy told four-year-old Hillary about a neighborhood bully, "you have my permission to hit her back.

You have to stand up for yourself. There's no room in this house for cowards."

The need to project an image of power at the expense of one's true feelings is characteristic of narcissistic personalities. And the home of Hugh and Dorothy Rodham was the perfect breeding ground for a narcissist like Hillary, who grew up feeling entitled to get away with things that others could not.

In all cases of narcissism, noted Doctor Otto F. Kernberg, a leading expert on the subject of borderline personality organization and narcissistic pathology, there is "a parental figure, usually the mother or mother surrogate, who functions well on the surface in a superficially well-organized home, but with a degree of callousness, indifference, and nonverbalized spiteful aggression.... Sometimes it was…the cold hostile mother's narcissistic use of the child which made [her] 'special,' set [her] off on the road in search of compensatory admiration and greatness."

Hillary had been traveling that road all her life. She chose a career in politics, despite the fact that in most essential respects she was unsuited for the life of a politician.

When she was nineteen years old and a student at Wellesley College, she wrote a friend and confessed that she was a misanthrope who disliked people and avoided their company.

"Can you be a misanthrope and still love some individuals?" she asked in her letter. "How about a compassionate misanthrope?"

"When the stress of college life became too much, she would fantasize about living a life of 'withdrawn simplicity,' preferably in some quiet place where she could devote herself to helping others and reading books," Jeff Gerth and Don Van Natta wrote in *Her Way: The Hopes and Ambitions of Hillary Rodham Clinton*. "But Hillary knew such work required a love of being with people and profound patience, and she was not a natural at either."

Hillary never cured herself of her misanthropy. In that regard, she resembled other famous liberal misanthropes, such as her heroine Eleanor Roosevelt and the Indian independence leader Mohandas Gandhi.

The British historian Andrew Roberts once described the Mahatma as "the archetypal...progressive intellectual, professing his love for mankind as a concept while actually despising people as individuals."

That was as good a description of Hillary as anyone had come up with yet.

—

There was no need to feel sorry for Hillary; many people suffered far worse childhoods than hers. But Hillary's upbringing did provide a clue to why she turned out to be so unlikeable.

"You can argue that there is a repetition compulsion in Hillary's relationship with her husband," Doctor Robert Cancro, the former chairman of the Psychiatry Department of New York University Langone Medical Center, told the author of this book. "Her marriage to Bill Clinton is a kind of microcosm of her relationship with her father, who was also a domineering, narcissistic kind of guy."

"In her personal life, she's always seemed like she had something to hide," Bill Clinton's former press secretary, Dee Dee Myers, said. "She had a difficult father, and she spent a lot of time trying to create an image of a functional family when she could have just said, 'It's my family.' The burden of perfection was upon her, and she carried it into her marriage. There's always this fear of letting people see what they already know."

It was this fear of exposure and humiliation that led one of Hillary's biographers, Carl Bernstein, to note that she indulged in "subterfuge and eliding."

Put simply, it helped explain why she lied and always tried to cover up her lies.

And it also explained why all the likeability lessons in the world weren't going to change her and put a stop to those lies.

"When she's alone with a small group of friends she trusts, Hillary can be warm and pleasant," one of her acquaintances told the author. "But when she has to stand up in front of an audience of strangers, her suspicion and mistrust of people kicks in and her facial expressions and her body language reflect a deep psychological turbulence."

"She freely admits she's always had anger issues," another acquaintance said. "When she's annoyed by people, which is often, it shows. She's never suffered fools gladly. As far as she's concerned, politics is all about sucking up to people she considers beneath her and unworthy of sharing her space.

"She looks at her critics as a handful of nuts," this person continued. "Her outburst during the Senate committee hearing on Benghazi—'What difference does it make?'—was in total keeping with her pattern of behavior. Something snaps when she's under pressure and emotional stress. As much as anything else, Bill pushed the Spielberg likeability lessons on Hillary in order to avoid another meltdown like Benghazi when she hit the campaign trail."

CHAPTER 6

"I'VE ALWAYS BEEN A YANKEES FAN"

*She went to the Yankees so that she could run for senator
from New York. It's so obvious. Why is she—doesn't she
know she looks like a fraud?*
—*Chris Matthews,* Hardball

For as long as Hillary had been in the public eye, her advisers had been trying to give her a makeover. At times, she cooperated with these Pygmalions, but more often than not she resisted their efforts to transform her into someone more pleasant and likeable.

But whether she chose to cooperate or not, the makeovers never stuck.

During Bill Clinton's 1992 presidential campaign, his top pollsters, Celinda Lake and Stan Greenberg, issued a confidential memo identifying "voters' discomfort with Hillary." Voters admired the strength of the Clinton marriage, they wrote, but "they also fear that only someone too politically ambitious, too strong, and too ruthless could survive such controversy so well. What voters find slick in Bill, they find ruthless in Hillary."

What Lake and Greenberg wrote about Hillary almost a quarter of a century ago could just as easily be written about her today:

> [Voters] perceive a political ruthlessness in her that is reinforced by their image of Bill Clinton. As one voter put it, "She knows what she wants and will do anything to get it."
>
> Women have their own contradictions and insecurities about the many roles they fulfill, which heighten their ambivalence about Hillary's life. They wonder whether Hillary shares their values or understands their lives.

In the spring of 1993, four months after Hillary and Bill moved into the White House, the journalist Michael Kelly wrote an article for the *New York Times Magazine* titled "Saint Hillary." In it, Kelly quoted Hillary as saying that she had grown tired of trying to be like Mother Teresa.

"I know that no matter what I did—if I did nothing, if I spent my entire day totally disengaged from what was going on around me—I'd be criticized for that," Hillary complained. "I mean, it's a no-win deal, no matter what I do, or try to do."

Two years later, in 1995, Hillary's press secretary, Lisa Caputo, presented several ideas to make Hillary more appealing, including a guest shot on a popular television sitcom. *"Home Improvement* is the most popular television show on the air," Caputo wrote. "They are willing to do a show on women, children and [family] issues or a show on whatever issues Hillary would like. The out-reach would be enormous and it would present Hillary in a very likeable light I believe."

A year after that, in 1996, when Hillary's polling numbers tanked and she was at the nadir of her term as first lady, she hired Michael Sheehan, Washington's top media-training guru. Sheehan was tasked with helping Hillary with an image makeover and with prepping her for the tour of her upcoming book, *It Takes a Village.*

On Thanksgiving Day of that same year, Hillary phoned Diane Blair, a professor of political science at the University of Arkansas and one of Hillary's closest friends. The two women spoke for nearly an hour. Later, Blair wrote an account in her diary of Hillary's self-pitying rant:

> "I'm a proud woman." "I'm not stupid; I know I should do more to suck up to the press, I know it confuses people when I change my hairdos, I know I should pretend not to have any opinions—but I'm just not going to. I'm used to winning and I intend to win on my own terms." "I know how to compromise, I have compromised, I gave up my name, got contact lenses, but I'm not going to try to pretend to be somebody that I'm not." I'm a complex person and they're just going to have to live with that.

In 1999, Hillary's staff sent her a memo urging her to be "real."

In 2000, Hillary turned again to the media-training expert Michael Sheehan. This time he tried to work his magic during her race for the U.S. Senate seat from New York being vacated by Daniel Patrick Moynihan. But Liz Moynihan, the senator's formidable wife, who managed all of his political campaigns, was less than impressed with Hillary's latest makeover.

"She's duplicitous," Liz told the author of this book. "She would say or do anything that would forward her ambitions. She can look you straight in the eye and lie, and sort of not know she's lying. Lying isn't a sufficient word; it's distortion—distorting the truth to fit the case."

Liz Moynihan wasn't alone in calling Hillary a fabulist who concocted dishonest stories. The New York media had a field day when Senate candidate Hillary, who hailed from Chicago and had always rooted for the Chicago Cubs, donned a Yankee baseball cap and declared in a *Today* show interview with Katie Couric: "The fact is, I've always been a Yankees fan."

Members of the New York press corps weren't the only ones who were on to Hillary. Female participants in the campaign's focus-group sessions described Hillary as "cunning," "pushy," and "cold." Complained one woman: "We really don't know who Hillary Clinton is."

Her eight years as a senator only served to solidify Hillary's reputation as a shameless hypocrite. With her eye firmly fixed on the White House, she put aside her left-wing convictions and demonstrated a newfound flair for bipartisanship. By her third year in the Senate, she had already sponsored bills with more than thirty-six Republicans.

To avoid being branded a liberal, she Vaselined her image to the point where the old left-wing Hillary was almost unrecognizable. She cosponsored a bill to criminalize flag burning. And, most famously of all, she voted in favor of the Iraq war in 2002 (when it was popular) before she voted against it in 2007 (when it wasn't).

"Hillary told [Obama] that her opposition to the [2007] surge in Iraq had been political," an appalled Robert Gates, the former secretary of defense, wrote in his memoir, *Duty*.

In 2008, a stiff and charmless Hillary was pitted against a loose and charismatic newcomer named Barack Hussein Obama for their party's presidential nomination. Her epic battle against Obama in Iowa and New Hampshire brought the issue of her unlikeability out of the shadows of confidential campaign memos and closed-door focus groups and to widespread public attention.

CHAPTER 7

A NEAR-DEATH EXPERIENCE

*I have learned the difference between a cactus and
a caucus. On a cactus, the pricks are on the outside.*
—*The late congressman Mo Udall*

Oprah Winfrey delivered the first blow to Hillary in Iowa.
For as long as anyone could remember, Oprah had been known as the "Queen of All Media." But to many of her fans, especially those on the Left, Oprah was more than that. In their eyes, she was the "Queen of Everything"—the doyenne of America's self-absorbed, secular, redistributive, and politically correct culture.

Over the years, Hillary had worked hard to ingratiate herself with this powerful cultural figure. She sent Oprah handwritten notes, birthday greetings, and invitations to special Clinton events. Oprah had never endorsed a political candidate, and in the months leading up to the Iowa caucuses of 2008, Hillary expected that Oprah's support for her would be understated—perhaps a nice spread in O, *the Oprah Magazine* and a couple of well-timed touchy-feely appearances on Oprah's TV show.

But in a dramatic break with precedent, Oprah ditched Hillary and endorsed Barack Obama for president. Her endorsement garnered headlines all over America.

To explain her decision, Oprah appeared on *Larry King Live*. The irrepressible King could hardly wait to ask the Queen if she had put her money where her mouth was.

"Well," replied Oprah, who was a mega-millionaire, "the truth of the matter is, whether I contribute or not contribute, you are limited to how much you [can] contribute, so my money isn't going to make any difference to him. I think that my value to him, my support of him, is probably worth more than any check."

That turned out to be the understatement of the election season. A study by two Maryland economists later concluded that Oprah's endorsement of Obama was worth more than one million votes in the primary race and put him over the top.

It was no secret that Oprah wanted to see an African American in the Oval Office. But her rationale for backing Obama went beyond race. The fact was, Oprah had never forgotten—nor forgiven—how she was dissed when Bill and Hillary were in the White House.

In an interview for this book, a close Oprah friend explained why Oprah still carried a grudge against the Clintons.

On May 7, 1999, two of President Clinton's senior White House advisers, Richard Socarides and Minyon Moore, exchanged memos about Oprah with the following derogatory subject line: "The fat lady hasn't sung yet."

The memos were distributed to Elena Kagan, deputy director of the Domestic Policy Council and a future justice of the Supreme Court; Neera Tanden, senior policy adviser to First Lady Hillary Clinton; and Bruce Lindsey, deputy counsel to President Clinton.

None of the recipients of the memos thought to object to the slur against Oprah.

Oprah had sources in the Clinton White House who told her about the offending "fat lady" memo.

"People in the Clinton administration desperately wanted Oprah to back certain presidential initiatives and lend her support to legislation, and when she showed a reluctance to do so, they joked 'the fat lady hasn't sung yet,'" explained one of Oprah's closest friends who was intimately acquainted with her thinking. "It's not that she isn't aware that people make fun of her weight and define her as being a heavy person. She certainly is aware of it and, for the most part, ignores it.

"But it is a different thing to have a slur about her weight written as the subject line of a memo that is circulated in the White House," the friend continued. "It doesn't matter that Hillary and Bill's fingerprints weren't on the memo. In Oprah's opinion, members of the Clinton administration wouldn't have used phrases like that if they thought the president and first lady would find it offensive.

"That wasn't the only reason Oprah never warmed to Hillary. But it was one of the many slights that distanced her from

Hillary. She thought Hillary was a user and not a particularly trustworthy person. Oprah always kept her at arm's length. I'm sure Hillary will make an approach to get Oprah's support in the 2016 election, but I'm just as sure she won't get it."

———

The second blow to fall on Hillary in 2008 came from another sort of royalty—*Hollywood* royalty in the form of the Dream-Works SKG trio of Steven Spielberg, Jeffrey Katzenberg, and David Geffen.

Everyone in Hollywood was under the impression that the SKGs were FOBs—Friends of Bill. That is, until Geffen, who was worth $6 billion, threw a fund-raiser for Barack Obama in the sprawling ten-acre backyard of his Beverly Hills mansion.

Geffen and his friends raised $1.3 million for Obama.

But that wasn't the worst of it as far as Hillary was concerned.

Afterward, Geffen agreed to sit for a rare on-the-record interview with his homegirl *New York Times* columnist Maureen Dowd. The interview took place at his home, the fabulous old Jack Warner estate on Angelo Drive. On display in the 13,600-square-foot mansion were paintings by famous American artists, which were valued at $1.1 billion, making it the most valuable private art collection in the world. The home also featured a curiosity that was tailor-made for a Hollywood mogul—the floor on which Napoleon was standing when he proposed to Josephine.

Normally, Geffen played his cards close to the vest, but he couldn't restrain himself when he started venting about the Clintons.

"It's not a very big thing to say, 'I made a mistake' on the [Iraq] war, and typical of Hillary Clinton that she can't," Geffen said. "She's so advised by so many smart advisers who are covering every base. I think that America was better served when the candidates were chosen in smoke-filled rooms."

Most people outside Geffen's inner circle didn't know that he had parted company with Bill and Hillary several years before the Dowd interview.

In the final hours of the Clinton administration, Bill granted 177 presidential pardons. One of them went to bank swindlers Edgar and Vonna Jo Gregory. It was later learned that Tony Rodham, Hillary's younger brother, had received a "consultant's fee" to arrange the Gregory pardon.

Another pardon went to the fugitive Marc Rich, an international commodities trader who had fled to Switzerland to avoid being prosecuted on charges of tax evasion. The pardon was viewed in many circles as a flagrant payoff to Rich's former wife, Denise, who had contributed more than $100,000 to Hillary's Senate campaign and $450,000 to the Clinton Library.

At the same time that Bill was letting the Gregorys and Rich go scot-free, Geffen—who was also a major Democratic Party donor—was lobbying the president to grant a pardon to Leonard Peltier. A Native American activist, Peltier was serving two consecutive terms of life imprisonment for first-degree murder in the shooting of two FBI agents. Many in Hollywood and beyond believed that Peltier had been wrongly convicted, and Geffen was joined in his appeal for a pardon by Nelson Mandela and the Dalai Lama as well as by such smooth operators as Archbishop Desmond Tutu and the Reverend Jesse Jackson.

Clinton ignored Geffen's request.

And as anyone in Hollywood could tell you, you didn't cross David Geffen without paying a price.

The Dowd interview was Geffen's payback.

"Marc Rich getting pardon?" Geffen scoffed. "An oil-profiteer expatriate who left the country rather than pay taxes or face justice? Yet another time when the Clintons were unwilling to stand for the things that they genuinely believe in. Everybody in politics lies, but they do it with such ease, it's troubling."

When that phrase—*"they do it [lie] with such ease, it's troubling"*—appeared in black and white in Dowd's column, it ricocheted from coast to coast and instantly became part of political lore. It was a reminder of William Safire's famous opening sentence about Hillary in a 1996 *Times* column: "Americans of all political persuasions are coming to the sad realization that our First Lady—a woman of undoubted talents who was a role model for many in her generation—is a congenital liar."

———

By early December 2007, Barack Obama had captured the lead in the Iowa polls, and Oprah Winfrey was drawing record crowds at Obama campaign rallies.

Panic broke out among Hillary's donors. Rumors began flying of a shake-up in her unruly and famously unmanageable staff. Reporters started writing eulogies for Hillary's campaign.

Hillary responded by calling in the cavalry: Bill Clinton.

With the presidential caucuses just two weeks away, she and Bill started making joint appearances at coffee shops and diners all across Iowa. She dropped her objection to using her mother, Dorothy, and daughter, Chelsea, in TV commercials. And just before Christmas, she embarked on what a *New York Times* headline writer with a droll sense of humor described as a "Likability Tour."

This is how the *Times* played it: "Mrs. Clinton has embarked this week on a warm-and-fuzzy tour, blitzing full throttle by helicopter across Iowa to present herself as likable and heartwarming, a complement to her 'strength and experience' message that the campaign felt a female candidate needed first."

After Hillary lost to Obama in Iowa (she came in third after Obama and John Edwards), she mused about the outcome of the campaign.

"Maybe," she said, "they just don't like me."

There was no *maybe* about it.

▬

When Hillary got to New Hampshire, the site of the first primary in the nation, she reverted to form. She was spitting mad over her loss to Obama in Iowa, and she was eager to demonstrate that she wasn't intimidated by Obama's Chicago-style brass-knuckles politics. As her mother, Dorothy, might have said: "There's no room in this campaign for cowards."

During their final debate in the Granite State, Hillary came across as defensive and angry—her old default expression when speaking in public.

"Making change is not about what you believe, it's not about a speech you make," she said, taking a shot at Obama, a first-term U.S. senator who, she believed, was riding on a smile and a shoe-shine and a lot of hot air.

The moderator caught Hillary's negative vibes and asked about her "personality deficit."

How would she respond to voters who thought Obama was more likeable than she was?

"Well," she replied, "that hurts my feelings, but I'll try to go on."

Then she turned to Obama and added, "He's very likeable. I agree with that. I don't think I'm *that* bad."

But Obama wouldn't let Hillary off the hook.

"You're likeable enough, Hillary," he said, throwing her some shade.

Hillary's camp complained that Obama had been cruel and insensitive. He wouldn't have used such a patronizing phrase if his opponent were a man. Hillary accused him of being "sexist"—her automatic fallback position whenever someone criticized her.

But the S-word didn't seem to damage Obama, for within forty-eight hours, he had piled up a double-digit lead in the polls.

It looked like a repeat of Iowa.

Toward the end of the New Hampshire campaign, Hillary found herself in a small Portsmouth café, answering questions from sixteen undecided voters, most of them women.

"My question is very personal, how do you do it?" asked Marianne Pernold Young, a freelance photographer. "How do you, how do you...keep upbeat and so wonderful?"

Facing the likely prospect of defeat, Hillary indulged her penchant for self-pity.

"You know," she said, tearing up, "this is very personal for me."

This wasn't the first time a candidate for the Democratic nomination appeared to cry during a New Hampshire primary campaign. Edmund Muskie, the former governor of Maine and an early favorite for his party's nod in 1972, was reported to have tears streaming down his face while he stood in a snowstorm and delivered a speech defending his wife. As a result, Muskie was attacked as a crybaby and his candidacy was doomed.

Some critics said Hillary's tears were phony. But whether genuine or not, it didn't seem to matter. When Hillary turned on the waterworks, the liberal media hailed her for being brave and for revealing her "personal" side.

"The feminist debate that raged two decades ago will henceforth be settled in favor of crying," Timothy Noah wrote, tongue in cheek, in Slate, an online magazine.

Against all the odds and expectations, the newly "humanized" Hillary won in New Hampshire. When one of her aides congratulated her on the victory, Hillary said, "I get really tough when people fuck with me."

She mounted a fierce, five-month-long battle against Obama. After she lost to Obama in the Maine caucuses, she went negative, launching a blistering series of attack ads against Obama that appealed to white working-class voters and racialized the campaign.

In the end, Hillary racked up nearly eighteen million primary votes, virtually tying Obama in the popular-vote total. But Obama defeated her in the arena that counted: convention delegates. Obama won 2,285½ delegates to Hillary's 1,973.

Obama declared victory on June 3, 2008.

Hillary refused to concede.

Her mother had told her never to back down. Her father had taught her to have a hide like a rhinoceros.

Hillary threatened to contest the nomination right up to the Democratic Party's August convention.

Finally, after four days of kvetching and carrying on, she threw in the towel.

—

Hillary viewed her near-death experience in the January 2008 New Hampshire Democratic presidential primary as a critical turning point in her political life. In her opinion, it proved she could come from behind and connect with voters and be a credible national candidate.

Through the long years of the Obama presidency, it was her experience in New Hampshire that kept alive her determination to run again for president.

And memories of victory in New Hampshire helped to bring her full circle to the presidential campaign of 2016—this time around as a candidate with no killer challenger in her own party. Instead, she would have a projected $2 billion war chest, a massive data-driven ground operation, a liberal media lusting for a female president, and most demographic trends in her favor.

But Hillary also entered the 2016 presidential campaign with a boatload of baggage—a tissue-thin résumé as a U.S. senator and secretary of state, a Vesuvius of scandals, widespread Clinton fatigue, a reputation for mendacity, no clear rationale for her candidacy, a brawler's reputation for foreign interventions, and a forbidding personality.

Chuck Schumer, her former Senate colleague from New York, called her "the most opaque person you'll ever meet in your life."

Many top Democrats in Iowa, site of the first-in-the-nation caucuses, were put off by her unlikeability.

"Elizabeth Warren, I could enjoy going out to lunch with her. Hillary less," said Lorraine Williams, the chairwoman of Iowa's Washington County Democrats.

In recent years, candidates who succeeded in capturing the White House—Ronald Reagan, Bill Clinton, George W. Bush, and Barack Obama—have all had one thing in common: a compelling personality that inspired millions of people to trust them.

Hillary Clinton is missing that chip.

She is the polar opposite of charismatic.

She can only *pretend* to be likeable.

PART III

A PANTSUIT-WEARING GLOBETROTTER

Clinton presented [Russian foreign minister Sergei] Lavrov with a gift-wrapped red button, which said "Reset" in English and "Peregruzka" in Russian. The problem was, "peregruzka" doesn't mean reset. It means overcharged, or overloaded. And Lavrov called her out on it. "We worked hard to get the right Russian word. Do you think we got it?" Clinton asked Lavrov. "You got it wrong," Lavrov said.
—**FoxNews.com**

CHAPTER 8

THE PRAETORIAN GUARD

*I have made more friends for American culture than the
State Department. Certainly I have made fewer enemies,
but that isn't very difficult.*
—*Playwright Arthur Miller*

A natural tension exists between all new secretaries of state
and the career Foreign Service officers who run Foggy
Bottom's bureaus and its embassies, consulates, and diplomatic missions around the world. That tension is normally smoothed over by incoming secretaries who show a decent
respect for the opinion of the permanent bureaucracy and ask for
help to find their way around.

Not so Hillary Clinton.

On her first day on the job in January 2009, Hillary came
striding confidently down the State Department's seventh-floor
gallery, which was hung with oil portraits of her predecessors
going back to the first secretary of state, Thomas Jefferson. She

looked for all the world, as one staffer recalled, "like the capo di tutti i capi, the boss of bosses, trying to intimidate everyone in sight."

Her heels clicked in unison with two made members of her political family—Huma Abedin, her deputy chief of staff, and Cheryl Mills, her chief of staff—who marched in lockstep behind Hillary and flanked her on the right and left.

Mills was Hillary's Tom Hagen, the Godfather's consigliere. She represented her boss in all matters.

A Stanford Law School graduate, Mills had earned a place in the Clinton inner circle when, as associate White House counsel, she delivered a passionate legal defense of Bill Clinton during his 1999 impeachment trial in the U.S. Senate. She was a senior adviser to Hillary's 2008 presidential campaign, was a member of the board of the Clinton Foundation, and was a key player in some of the Clintons' cover-ups.

As Hillary's chief of staff at the State Department, according to the *Wall Street Journal*, Mills "told State Department records specialists she wanted to see all documents requested on the controversial Keystone XL pipeline, and later demanded that some be held back."

"In another case," the *Journal* also reported, "Ms. Mills's staff negotiated with the records specialists over the release of documents about former President Bill Clinton's speaking engagements—also holding some back."

The seventh-floor staff soon learned to expect big trouble whenever Cheryl Mills and Huma Abedin were summoned to

Hillary's inner sanctum. These two women—along with Hillary's attack-dog press secretary Philippe Reines and her chief policy adviser Jake Sullivan—made up Hillary's praetorian guard at the State Department. They understood that Hillary viewed her term as secretary of state as a stepping stone to the White House, and they did everything in their power to shelter Hillary from controversy.

"Important policy papers that had been worked on for months before Hillary took over and that ran the slightest bit of risk were ignored, gutted, or tossed out without explanation by her staff," said a longtime Foreign Service officer who was interviewed for this book. "It soon became apparent that Hillary's people were going to turn the place upside down and try to micromanage everything to save Hillary's ass."

In the past, most secretaries of state presided over large inclusive meetings where major issues were on the table and members of the senior staff were encouraged to express their opinions openly.

Not so Hillary Clinton.

Only Huma, Cheryl, Philippe, and Jake were in on everything. And Hillary outsourced politically risky assignments to special envoys. Veteran diplomat Richard Holbrooke was in charge of winding down the war in Afghanistan by cobbling together a political settlement with the Taliban. And former U.S. senator George Mitchell was sent to the Middle East to knock heads and make peace between the Israelis and the Palestinians.

Both missions failed.

—

While Hillary was at Foggy Bottom, she usually worked from ten in the morning until ten at night. Like the policy wonk that she was, she often got lost in minutiae. She read every paper down to the last dreary detail and went over and over the most routine memos until she drove her staff to distraction.

"She clearly didn't think the career Foreign Service officers took her seriously," a diplomat said in an interview for this book. "And that went double for the White House. Hillary had a giant chip on her shoulder and was furious that she wasn't treated fairly by the Obamas."

Hillary's biggest beef was with Valerie Jarrett, senior adviser to the president, and the woman who, after Michelle Obama, had President Obama's ear. Obama would make important foreign policy decisions, and Jarrett—the real power behind the presidential throne—would implement them, without bothering to pass them by Hillary or give her a heads-up.

In a typical case, Hillary discovered that the White House was conducting secret back-channel discussions with the Castro brothers in Cuba in an effort to normalize relations with that Communist country. Hillary called Valerie Jarrett and complained that the State Department was once again being left in the dark.

Jarrett wouldn't let Hillary get a word in edgewise. Finally, in frustration, Hillary held the telephone receiver at arm's length so that everyone in the room could hear Jarrett talking. While the staff listened, Hillary silently mouthed Jarrett's words, mimicking her agitated behavior.

On most nights after work, Hillary would ask an aide to bring her a Michelob Ultra, her favorite low-carb beer. Then she'd put her feet up on her desk, take a swig from the bottle, and start imitating the voices of world leaders.

She was a talented impersonator. Her specialty was the swaggering Vladimir Putin. And she did a wicked impersonation of Bill Clinton, down to his seductive croak.

CHAPTER 9

SHAFTED

Even a paranoid has some real enemies.
—Henry Kissinger

D espite the best efforts of her praetorian guard, Hillary never felt secure in her role as secretary of state. She suspected that everything she said was leaked to the media. She was convinced that Valerie Jarrett had installed moles in the State Department and that these spies were ratting her out to members of the White House staff, who were still nursing a grudge against Hillary from the bitterly fought days of the 2008 Democratic primary campaign.

Her paranoia often got the better of her. She would order high-ranking deputies and undersecretaries to leave the room in the middle of meetings because she suspected them of being spies.

She was tense and irritable most of the time, and there were frequent eruptions of her famous temper, just as there had been when she was a U.S. senator and indulged in shouting matches with Chuck Schumer, her colleague from New York. Loud arguments became the norm at the State Department, not only during Hillary's staff meetings, but while she was walking down the corridors and riding in the elevators. You could hear her coming a mile away.

"I've been at State since the mid-1980s, and I've never seen such acrimony," said a Foreign Service officer. "I had heard stories about Hillary's problems with anger management, but I didn't believe them until I saw them with my own eyes. After a telephone argument with Valerie Jarrett, Hillary threw a heavy water glass across her office and sent shards flying.

"Another time," this person continued, "after a telephone argument with President Obama, she took her right arm and cleared off her small working desk, sending pictures, glasses, everything crashing to the floor.

"The two times when she fainted [while boarding a plane in Yemen in 2011 and working in her office in 2012] were periods of stress brought on by furious arguments.

"After the episode with President Obama, I heard her tell Huma, 'I don't want Bill to hear anything about this.'"

———

Before she became secretary of state, Hillary had spent a great deal of time discussing with Bill the pros and cons of

Obama's offer. She was suspicious of Obama's motives and skeptical that he would allow her to put her stamp on foreign policy.

"I don't want to be a pantsuit-wearing globetrotter," Hillary told Bill in the presence of several friends.

To allay her fears, Bill asked his right-hand man, Doug Band, to negotiate an agreement with the White House. A "memorandum of understanding" was drafted and signed by both Clintons and by the White House counsel. The memorandum stipulated that Hillary would have a free hand to choose her own deputies and run the State Department as she saw fit. In return, Hillary agreed that the Clinton Foundation would not accept contributions from foreign donors as long as she was at Foggy Bottom, and that Bill would seek the Obama administration's approval of all his speeches.

Bill agreed to these stringent conditions because he saw the State Department job as an important station on Hillary's march to the White House. It would allow her to remain in the public eye during Obama's term in office and give her an opportunity to fill in her résumé as a woman who had the grit to deal with the world's toughest male leaders.

Bill had grandiose plans for Hillary: she would make peace between Israel and the Palestinians, open a dialogue with North Korea, bring pressure to bear on Iran, and force the ayatollahs to end their nuclear program.

Who knew? She might even end up with the Nobel Peace Prize.

There was only one problem with Bill's vision for his wife. It turned out that Hillary's paranoia about her enemies in the Obama White House was well founded.

Chief among the enemies were members of the triumvirate that ruled from the Oval Office—Barack Obama, Valerie Jarrett, and Michelle Obama. They never intended to let Hillary run foreign policy.

In her confrontations with Hillary, Jarrett had a formidable army to back her up: Chief of Staff Rahm Emanuel, Press Secretary Robert Gibbs, and chief political adviser David Axelrod. Denis McDonough, a foreign policy adviser who ultimately replaced Emanuel as the president's chief of staff, referred to Hillary as "the principle *implementer*" of policy, *not* its architect.

Hillary was forced to assume the role she had most wanted to avoid—a pantsuit-wearing globetrotter. As one official told *Politico*, Hillary practiced "odometer diplomacy," with "a focus on globetrotting to bolster America's relationships abroad coupled with attempts to cope with an array of pop-up crises."

When Caroline Kennedy was appointed ambassador to Japan, she asked Hillary what she could expect when she took up her post in Tokyo.

"Don't expect to get your real marching orders from State," Hillary told Caroline. "The way the Obama government works, everything important in foreign policy comes from the White House. And Valerie [Jarrett] pretty much runs the show down there. You'll feel Valerie breathing down your neck all the way to Tokyo. She's going to have a lot to say about how you represent our country in Japan, and believe me, she won't be shy about it."

━━

Hillary had extracted a promise from Obama that she would be free to choose her own deputies, but that was not how things worked out.

With Obama's approval, Jarrett insisted that Hillary hire James Steinberg as her deputy secretary of state. Although Steinberg had once worked in the Clinton administration, Hillary did not like him. But the White House left her no choice, and she brought Steinberg on board as her deputy.

Hillary and Steinberg often clashed on major issues of policy. He seemed to enjoy thumbing his nose at Hillary. In the end, however, she won the bureaucratic wrestling match. The unhappy Steinberg lasted just two years at Foggy Bottom before he handed in his resignation and became dean of the Maxwell School of Citizenship and Public Affairs at Syracuse University.

The Steinberg episode was just one in a multitude of humiliations inflicted on Hillary by the White House.

For example, Hillary would be summoned to the White House for a meeting only to discover when she arrived that the meeting had been canceled without anyone bothering to tell her.

"I arrived for the 10:15 mtg and was told there was no mtg," she e-mailed aides in 2009. "This is the second time this has happened. What's up???"

Other times, she was left in the dark about the timing of cabinet meetings.

"I heard on the radio," Hillary wrote in an e-mail on June 8, 2009, "that there is a Cabinet mtg this am. Is there? Can I go? If not, who are we sending?"

Old State Department hands said they had to reach far back in their memory to recall a relationship between the White House and State Department that was so one-sided in favor of the president. They concluded that only Richard Nixon's secretary of state, William Pierce Rogers, had been shafted as badly as Hillary.

CHAPTER 10

DOUBLE DIPPING

*It would have been perfectly logical if [Huma Abedin]
had said, "I'm out of here." Any woman could have
understood that.*
—Huma Abedin's friend Rory Tahari

I t was the spring of 2012 and Secretary of State Hillary Clinton was on a late-night flight to Beijing.

As always, Huma Abedin, Hillary's longest-serving aide, was close at hand.

Huma was an attractive and stylish woman with a murky personal background. She was born in Kalamazoo, Michigan, and moved to Saudi Arabia with her Muslim parents when she was two years old. She grew up speaking English, Urdu (a language associated with the Muslim region of Hindustan), and Arabic.

She didn't return to America until her late teens, when she was admitted to George Washington University. There, she became a member of the executive board of the Muslim Students Association, which was founded by the Muslim Brotherhood, a radical Islamist group whose stated goal was to instill the Koran and Sunnah (a major source of Islamic law) as the "sole reference point for...ordering the life of the Muslim family, individual, community...and state."

As a college intern in 1996, Huma was assigned to the first lady's office in the Clinton White House, where she immediately came to the attention of Hillary.

For the next twelve years—from 1996 until 2008, when Hillary ran for the Democratic Party's presidential nomination—Huma wore two hats: she was Hillary's "body woman," her do-it-all personal assistant, and she was the assistant editor of the *Journal of Muslim Minority Affairs*. Her connection to that publication raised eyebrows in conservative circles, because the *Journal* was founded by Abdullah Omar Naseef, a notorious financier of Osama bin Laden and al Qaeda.

Huma's Pakistani mother, Saleha Mahmood Abedin, served as a representative of the Muslim World League, a fundamentalist group, and became the editor in chief of the *Journal of Muslim Minority Affairs*. Some Islamist-watchers, like Frank J. Gaffney Jr., president of the Center for Security Policy, have written about Huma's "extensive ties to the Muslim Brotherhood...whose self-declared mission is 'destroying Western civilization from within.'"

As "Hillary's shadow," Huma kept tabs on Hillary's personal needs—lodging, transportation, meals, and snacks. She made sure Hillary was dressed appropriately for the weather. And she carried Hillary's BlackBerry, which would become a major prop in Hillary's e-mail drama.

Over the years, the two women developed a strong personal bond, and Huma rose in the ranks to become Hillary's deputy chief of staff. More than an aide, Huma was, with the exception of Bill and Chelsea, the closest person to Hillary. Hillary never went anywhere without Huma.

Despite Huma's twenty-year relationship with Hillary, she had managed to remain largely under the public radar until the spring of 2011, when her husband, Democratic congressman Anthony Weiner, was unmasked as a serial pervert who sent lewd photos of himself via Twitter.

During the ensuing scandal, which forced Weiner to resign from Congress, Hillary counseled the now-pregnant Huma on how to deal with her wayward husband—a subject on which Hillary was of course a world-class expert. Not surprisingly, she urged Huma to follow her example and save her marriage.

Huma listened to Hillary and stuck by the disgraced Weiner.

People said that Hillary treated Huma as an adopted daughter. But she went much further than that. Following Huma's maternity leave, Hillary allowed her to continue drawing a State Department salary of $135,000 as a "special government employee" while at the same time she sat on the board of the Clinton Foundation and worked as a $355,000-a-year outside adviser to Teneo, a strategic consulting firm founded by Doug Band, himself a former adviser to President Bill Clinton.

Huma's double dipping was certainly unethical if not downright illegal. Some people speculated that Huma needed the money because Anthony Weiner was out of a job and broke. Others said she needed the dough to support her pricey lifestyle, which included designer frocks by Oscar de la Renta, Catherine Malandrino, and Prada, and handbags by Yves Saint Laurent. And some people said that Huma had simply caught the money bug from Hillary.

Huma's years of loyal service were richly rewarded when Hillary announced that she was running for president and anointed Huma as one of her chief surrogates.

"For all intents and purposes," a Clinton campaign aide told *Politico*, "[Huma is] No. 3 on the campaign, after [campaign chairman John] Podesta and [campaign manager Robby] Mook."

CHAPTER 11

"I LOVE YOU, BILLY"

*Those of us who follow politics seriously rather than
view it as a game show do not look at Hillary Clinton
and simply think "first woman president." We think—
for example—"first ex-co-president" or "first wife of a
disbarred lawyer and impeached former incumbent" or
"first person to use her daughter as photo-op protection
during her husband's perjury rap."*
—**Christopher Hitchens**

From the window of her Air Force C-32, a military version of the Boeing 757, Hillary could see the towering snow-covered mountain peaks of the Karakoram Range.

She picked up a phone and asked to be connected to her husband, who was thousands of miles away on a flight of his own in a G650 private jet. Their conversation took place on a speakerphone in the presence of Huma and State Department aides. One of the aides was later interviewed for this book.

"What are you up to?" Bill asked.

"I'm sitting here in my green bathrobe and eating cantaloupe," Hillary said.

Bill laughed and then fell silent.

Hillary was calling Bill about her trip to China. She rarely made a major decision without consulting him. No matter where in the world she might be, she'd pick up the phone and call him. But Bill's need to cover up his secret life made him cagey, and Hillary always had to drag details out of him.

As usual, he didn't offer any information about where he was and what he was up to—even though this time he wasn't up to his usual hijinks. He was headed to a Clinton Foundation conference on drugs used to fight AIDS.

In contrast to Bill, Hillary was open and shared every nuance of her life with her husband. She wanted him to know where she was going and what she was doing. And she wanted his input. Not that she took marching orders from Bill. On the contrary, when they spoke, she'd present the problem, usually get into a shouting match with him over what to do, and then come to her own conclusions.

Bill had given her a policy paper, prepared by a China expert, on Beijing's relationship with North Korea, Japan, and Hong Kong. It included specific recommendations on trade, human rights, democracy in Hong Kong, and other pressing issues in East Asia.

"I ran the list by the White House," Hillary told Bill over the speakerphone, "and they haven't responded."

"Screw them!" Bill said. "Just go ahead and present the proposals when you get to China. Once you do, they [the White House] can't very well take them back. *Make things happen.*"

Bill was outraged by the way people in the Obama White House treated his wife. In his view, they were not only rude and offensive; they were just plain stupid. They were wasting a valuable resource in Hillary. Obama's team had no idea how to run foreign policy. They had no coherent foreign policy philosophy or comprehensive strategy. They were making things up as they went along. And they were screwing up at every turn.

Bill often expressed his contempt for Obama; it was he who first christened Obama "the Amateur," a name I adopted for the title of a book. But he was especially scathing in his comments about Valerie Jarrett. He urged Hillary to stand her ground with Jarrett.

But there wasn't much Hillary could do, since it was obvious that Jarrett was Obama's avatar.

"Don't you get it?" Hillary told Bill during their airplane-to-airplane phone call. "The whole idea is to marginalize me."

"I get it," he said.

"I wish you were president," she said.

"I wish *you* were," he said.

"I love you, Billy," she said.

And they hung up.

CHAPTER 12

TOP TEN

When voters are asked specific things [Hillary Clinton] did as secretary of state, they don't actually know anything.
"What did she accomplish that you consider significant as secretary of state?" Bloomberg's Mark Halperin asked a focus group of Iowa Democrats. The responses:
"I really can't name anything off the top of my head."
"Give me a minute. Give me two minutes."
"Umm … no."
—Washington Post, *May 20, 2015*

"**T**he Washington consensus," Danielle Pletka of the American Enterprise Institute said, "is that [Hillary] was enormously ineffective [as secretary of state]… [though] no one was quite sure whether she was ineffective because she wanted to avoid controversy or because she wasn't trusted by the president to do anything."

In either case, the question that begged to be answered was: Could Hillary point to *any* accomplishments during her four years as secretary of state?

With a tip of the hat to David Letterman, here is how I sum up Hillary's record.

TOP TEN REASONS HILLARY WANTS TO FORGET HER TIME AT FOGGY BOTTOM

Number 10: I busted my butt offering Russia a "reset," but I didn't know Putin would translate the word to mean he could reset the Soviet Union's old borders and seize control of Crimea.

Number 9: I talked Obama into getting rid of Gaddafi, but I didn't know those wild and crazy guys in Libya would let their country become a major breeding ground for the Islamic State.

Number 8: I "pivoted" to Asia, but I didn't know Beijing would pivot right back by launching an aircraft carrier in the South China Sea and scaring the hell out of America's friends.

Number 7: I refused to put Boko Haram on a list of foreign terror groups, but I didn't know those ingrates would continue to rape hundreds of women and girls in an effort to create a new generation of Islamist militants.

Number 6: I sent former CIA spook Frank Wisner to Cairo to persuade President Mubarak to step down in favor of an orderly transition to democracy, but Mubarak laughed Wisner out of the Heliopolis Palace.

Number 5: I vowed to restore "America's standing around the world," but our enemies heard me say, "America will just *stand around*" while they take advantage of us.

Number 4: I made a promise to Obama that the Clinton Foundation wouldn't take donations from foreigners while I was secretary of state, but these days who can tell a foreigner from a native-born American?

Number 3: I received a report about the deteriorating security situation in Benghazi from my secret agent Sidney Blumenthal, but who listens to someone whose conspiracy theories earned him the nickname "Grassy Knoll"?

Number 2: I used a personal e-mail address with the initials of my maiden name (hdr22@clintonemail.com), but I didn't know people would be surprised. After all, Hillary Diane Rodham has always been the real me—not "Mrs. Clinton."

And Number 1: I racked up nearly a million miles in the air as secretary of state, but it turned out to be harder than I thought to cash in the frequent-flier miles for a ticket to the White House.

PART IV

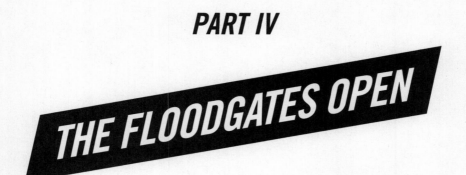

THE FLOODGATES OPEN

Eeh dah eeh dah
Ooooh, ooooh, ooooh
Scandal—now you've left me there's no healing the wounds
Hey scandal, and all the world can make us out to be fools
Here come the bad news, open the floodgates (oooh oooh)
They'll leave us bleeding
—Queen, "Scandal"

CHAPTER 13

"GET CAUGHT TRYING"

It is very comforting to believe that leaders who do terrible things are, in fact, mad. That way, all we have to do is make sure we don't put psychotics in high places and we've got the problem solved.
—**Tom Wolfe**, In Our Time

When Hillary left the State Department in February 2013, she moved her nascent presidential campaign into the Clinton Foundation's new offices in Manhattan's Time-Life Building. Once again, she linked her career to Bill's and made herself a hostage to fortune.

As in the past, Hillary and Bill talked frequently on the phone but rarely saw each other. He continued to rove about the world and spend much of his downtime at his library in Little Rock, where the foundation's nerve center was still located.

In the spring of 2013, the foundation was renamed for all three Clintons—Bill, Hillary, and Chelsea. This provided Chelsea with a cushy gig and gave her more say in the foundation's day-to-day operation. According to multiple sources, Chelsea's overbearing, I-know-better attitude rubbed people the wrong way, and many of the senior staff headed for the door.

As it happened, Chelsea was already doing well financially, thank you. She was a member of the board of IAC/InterActiveCorp, the digital media company run by Barry Diller, a longtime Clinton supporter. IAC/InterActiveCorp paid Chelsea $50,000 a year and granted her $250,000 in restricted stock. In addition, Chelsea pulled down a $600,000-a-year salary as a "special correspondent" for NBC News, doing feel-good segments for *Nightly News* and *Rock Center with Brian Williams*.

When *Politico* revealed Chelsea's NBC salary, the media went into overdrive poking fun at the arrangement. Business Insider calculated that Chelsea made $26,724 for every minute she was on-air. And the *Los Angeles Times* sniffed: "[Chelsea's assignment] raises the obvious question of NBC's goal in giving [her] a high-profile job and apparently paying her a top-echelon salary. The answer is equally obvious: Plainly, it was done to curry favor with the Clinton family."

———

Renaming the family business the Bill, Hillary & Chelsea Clinton Foundation couldn't have come at a worse time. For in August 2013, the *New York Times* unleashed the first in what would become a fusillade of accusations aimed at the heart of the foundation.

Noted the Gray Lady: "The Clinton Foundation [has] become a sprawling concern, supervised by a rotating board of old Clinton hands, vulnerable to distraction and threatened by conflicts of interest. It ran multimillion-dollar deficits for several years, despite vast amounts of money flowing in."

When Chelsea read the *New York Times* story, she went ballistic. She climbed into her Cadillac Escalade and drove from New York City to Chappaqua to confront her father.

It was a muggy weekend in mid-August, and Bill and Hillary had five or six people over for drinks. They had wandered over to Bill's office, where he was showing off his collection of African tribal masks, when Chelsea stormed into the barn, her face livid with anger.

"Inexcusable incompetence!" Chelsea shouted at her father, waving a copy of the *Times* article, which portrayed Doug Band, who was known as "Bill's adopted son," as the chief villain in the foundation's conflict-of-interest culture.

"Band has to go!" Chelsea screamed.

The guests shrank back against a far wall.

"I tried to give them space, but it was impossible not to hear most of what was said," recalled one of the guests who was interviewed for this book.

Chelsea told her father, "You treat these bastards like family, like your children, and you blindly trust them. They pay you back by screwing up the foundation's finances so badly it may be impossible to fix it. You assume that people are loyal because you are. But they are not. And this proves it."

"Everyone who was close to the Clintons knew that the foundation was hemorrhaging money and that Doug Band had a free hand," said the guest. "Chelsea hated Band. She hated the influence he had over her father, and she deeply resented the inference that he was somehow like a son to Bill. That really grated on her."

Chelsea walked out and slammed the door to Bill's office. She circled the garden a few times, and then came back in, still fuming.

Bill looked pale and stricken.

Hillary, on the other hand, looked pleased.

"She agreed with Chelsea and was proud of her daughter for facing up to her father," said the guest. "At that moment it became clear to me that if Bill wasn't exactly afraid of Chelsea, he was definitely in awe of her. I would have bet my last dollar that Chelsea was going to take over the foundation."

In August 2014, Chelsea announced she was leaving her six-figure job at NBC.

But that didn't alleviate the pain inside the Clinton family.

According to sources close to Hillary, the *Times* article and follow-up stories about the Clinton Foundation rocked the Clinton marriage more than anything since the Monica Lewinsky affair.

"Whenever Hillary gave Bill holy hell, she brought up the subject of his women, and this time was no exception," said a source. "She accused him of playing around with women in what she called his 'Little Rock love nest.' She complained about the millions spent on first-class tickets and noncommercial travel for beautiful women. She named names, including several movie stars like Dakota Fanning, who had traveled with Bill to Africa."

Chelsea joined her mother in criticizing the excesses and extravagance. Mother and daughter insisted that Bill get rid of his old cronies, including Bruce Lindsey, the former White House counsel and chairman of the board of the foundation, who still lived part-time in Arkansas.

Their arguments grew heated, with the three of them shouting at the same time. At one point, Chelsea pointed out that she had worked as a consultant at McKinsey & Company, the business management firm.

"I'm the only one in this family who's got any business experience," she shouted.

To which Bill reminded her that he had run a pretty big operation himself—the U.S. government.

"Bill was so rocked by their attack that he couldn't take it anymore, and he made arrangements to fly to Africa," said the source. "He simply got the hell out of town. But before he left, he agreed that Hillary and Chelsea could make whatever changes in the foundation they thought necessary. That was when the nerve center of the foundation was moved from his library in Little Rock to the Time-Life Building in New York City, where Chelsea could manage it."

Not long afterward, Chelsea got her wish about Doug Band. In June 2015, Bubba's money man and "surrogate son," as the *New York Post* referred to Band, resigned from the Clinton Foundation—a casualty of rubbing Chelsea Clinton the wrong way.

Chelsea was her mother's daughter in a number of ways. Like Hillary, she had a hair-trigger temper and flew into a rage at the slightest provocation. A taste of power only seemed to whet her appetite. And now that she had a big say in running the foundation, she had the urge to go into another part of the family business: book writing as a political art.

While pregnant, she began putting together a book titled *It's Your World: Get Informed, Get Inspired & Get Going*. The book, which was aimed at readers ages ten to fourteen, was due out in mid-September 2015, just as interest in the 2016 presidential primaries would begin to heat up. Chelsea was planning a major book tour, which she saw as an important adjunct to her mother's bid for the White House.

But Chelsea, like Hillary, had a tin political ear, and in a letter posted on her publisher's website, she made a big boo-boo: "We have a saying in my family," she wrote. "It's always better to get caught trying (rather than not try at all)."

Get caught trying!

Was that a Freudian slip?

Or was that the motto engraved on the Clinton family's coat of arms?

It was a saying, wrote Heather Wilhelm, a weekly columnist for RealClearPolitics, "that ranks right up there with 'There's more than one way to obliterate an old email server' and 'If the silverware is missing, Sandy Berger's pants are a-jangling.'"

At the same time that she was preparing her book for publication, Chelsea was urging her parents to find a role in the family foundation for her husband, Marc Mezvinsky.

"Since marrying Chelsea Clinton five years ago, Marc Mezvinsky, a money manager, appears to have settled into his life as Bill and Hillary Clinton's son-in-law," the *New York Times* reported. "He has regularly appeared at charitable events, once introducing the former president at the Clinton Foundation's celebrity poker tournament by dryly saying, 'You may have heard of my father-in-law.'"

Mezvinsky started raising money for his hedge fund, Eaglevale Partners, in 2011, barely a year after he married Chelsea in a wedding ceremony that was attended by some five hundred people, including former secretary of state Madeleine Albright; Democratic super-fund-raiser Terry McAuliffe; fashion designer Vera Wang; Anthony Weiner and Huma Abedin; Ted Danson and Mary Steenburgen; Chelsea's BFF Nicole Fox; Marc's father, Edward Mezvinsky, who spent eighty months in prison for bank, mail, and wire fraud; and Ghislaine Maxwell, who had attracted worldwide press attention for her relationship with convicted pedophile Jeffrey Epstein.

"Bill and Hillary were never enthusiastic about Chelsea's marriage to Marc," a close family friend said in an interview for this book. "They were uncomfortable with Marc's father's felony conviction and jail sentence. They knew it was unfair to blame Marc for the sins of his father, but the fact was the Mezvinsky family name was tainted and it left its stain on Chelsea.

"Bill and Hillary ran as far away as they could from Marc's parents," this source continued. "When Marc's mother Marjorie filed paperwork in 2013 to run in the Democratic primary for a congressional seat, Hillary and Bill showed her scant support.

"At first, Marc felt left out of the Clinton family. Bill and Hillary didn't pay him much attention. Personally, he wasn't their cup of tea. He's a brooding kind of guy, cerebral and soft-spoken, in contrast to Chelsea, who is upbeat and animated like her father.

"But when Chelsea announced she was pregnant in the spring of 2014, the Clintons' attitude toward Marc underwent a change. I was at a small dinner party at Chappaqua when Bill put his arm around Marc's shoulder and took him into his office for a long talk. They came out looking like best friends, so it was obvious that they had a breakthrough. Marc's name began appearing on Clinton Global Initiative–related things."

———

Marc was more than a friend of the family; he was a friend with benefits.

He met with a series of wealthy investors who had close ties to Bill and Hillary and apparently brought them closer still. The investors included Lloyd C. Blankfein, the CEO of Goldman Sachs, which had paid Bill $1.35 million for eight speeches. Another investor, hedge-fund manager Marc Lasry, was a major donor to Hillary's 2008 presidential campaign. A few years after Chelsea graduated from Stanford University, Lasry was more than happy to give her a job at his fund, Avenue Capital.

Investigative reporters at the *Times* dug up several other examples of Mezvinsky investors who had close relationships with Bill and Hillary.

"Rock Creek Group, a Washington-based investment advisory firm, placed $13 million from the California Public Employees' Retirement System and another public pension fund with Eaglevale in late 2011 and early 2012," the *Times* reported. "Rock Creek's chairwoman, Afsaneh Beschloss, attended state dinners at the Clinton White House in the late 1990s and was a panelist in the annual meeting of the Clinton Global Initiative."

After a dinner with Greece's prime minister, Mezvinsky bet big on a turnaround of the country's economy. He invested millions in Greek bank stocks and Greek debt. He lost his shirt—and the shirts of his investors—and in 2014 Eaglevale acknowledged, "Our recent predictions regarding Greek politics have proved incorrect."

"Investing in Greece is stupid," Larry Kudlow, an economist and a CNBC senior contributor, told the author of this book. "Doing it on the basis of a dinner with an ultra-weak prime minister who was a temporary figurehead is even stupider. Plus, the Clinton insiderism of the dinner, and the hedge fund's money raising, is so typically sleazy."

CHAPTER 14

IMAGINING "HILLARY 5.0"

*Hillary Clinton has enlisted a Coca-Cola marketing whiz
to help brand her expected presidential campaign.
This is quintessential Clinton. The most politically savvy
couple in America has a penchant for seeking out the
latest shiny toy, a magic bullet to make everything work.*
—Albert R. Hunt, Bloomberg View

In the weeks leading up to Hillary's announcement that she was running for president, her mansion at 3067 Whitehaven Street was the scene of feverish preparations.

Day after day, a whirl of experts passed through Whitehaven's Secret Service checkpoint, where world-famous economists, bow-tied academics, burly union bosses, political *machers*, and Democratic Party grandees were required to open their briefcases for inspection and, in some cases, endure full-body patdowns. The experts came from every quarter of the fractious Democratic Party, but most of them—like progressive economists Joseph Stiglitz and Alan Krueger—came from the Elizabeth Warren populist wing.

Hillary was shedding her reputation as a "centrist" and returning to her ideological roots on the Far Left. And no one— not even Elizabeth Warren—had more impressive credentials. As a twenty-something student at Yale Law School, Hillary had worked as a summer intern for the radical left-wing law firm Treuhaft, Walker and Burnstein, and befriended the leftist community organizer Saul Alinsky.

"It is easy to forget that for years, Mrs. Clinton weathered criticism that she was too liberal, the socialist foil to her husband's centrist agenda," noted the *New York Times*. "Economists in the Clinton administration referred to the first lady and her aides as 'the Bolsheviks.'"

Hillary's tutorials with the experts were usually held in Whitehaven's spacious dining room. She would show up looking tired and bedraggled and dressed in sweats or a muumuu. Visitors noticed that her hands visibly shook. She did not look healthy. Some came away from their encounter with Hillary wondering if she possessed the strength and vitality necessary for the demands of a nineteen-month-long political campaign.

She'd listen to the experts, ask questions, take notes, and then disappear through the French doors with a wave and a forced smile. No one could tell which of the advisers had scored a homerun with Hillary and which ones had struck out.

———

One of the first casualties of these meetings was the Spielberg likeability lessons.

Everyone agreed they weren't working.

"For more than a decade, Mrs. Clinton has tried to swat away a persistent concern about her ability to connect with voters," noted the *New York Times*. "'Saturday Night Live' recently captured that problem in a sketch featuring an actress playing Mrs. Clinton, who said of herself at one point, 'What a relatable laugh!' Years of security-infused Bubble Wrap around her travels and a wealthy lifestyle have done little to pull Mrs. Clinton closer to voters."

"Given that [Hillary] has been in public life since 1992, it's a bit incongruous to consider that her speaking style is often so lacking," wrote the *Washington Post*. "She has yet to master 'the big speech,' which is part of the toolbox of any major politician."

When Hillary spoke in public, she still had trouble making eye contact with her audience. Her eyes wandered from the text of her speech or her talking points to some unfocused spot on the ceiling and back again. Her voice was flat and uninflected. She was at her worst with members of the media; in the presence of journalists, she came across as scripted, charmless, and defensive.

"Her speaking style hasn't improved," wrote Sean Trende, the senior election analyst for RealClearPolitics. "If anything, she's lost a step from 2008."

In exasperation, Hillary quit taking the likeability lessons.

"I decided I had enough with the camera and the recordings and the coaches," Hillary told a friend. "I got so angry I knocked the fucking camera off its tripod. That was the end of my Stanislavski period."

—

Some of the biggest names in the world of corporate marketing strategy—Wendy Clark of Coca-Cola and Roy Spence of the Austin-based ad firm GSD&M—showed up at Whitehaven.

"People familiar with Clinton's preparations said Clark and Spence are focused on developing imaginative ways to 'let Hillary be Hillary,' as one person said, and help her make emotional connections with voters," reported the *Washington Post*. "Their job is to help imagine Hillary 5.0—the rebranding of a first lady turned senator turned failed presidential candidate turned secretary of state turned...2016 Democratic presidential nominee.... In their mission to present voters with a winning picture of their likely candidate, no detail is too big or small—from her economic opportunity agenda to the design of the 'H' in her future campaign logo."

When the new logo—a blue "H" with a rightward-facing red arrow—was unveiled in April 2015, it received a unanimous thumbs-down from art directors and graphic designers. The *New Yorker* ran a cartoon that showed two people gazing at a Hillary campaign poster with the "H" logo and a caption that read: "I'm just not entirely sure a big red arrow pointing right is the best logo for a Democratic candidate, is all."

Kristina Schake, Michelle Obama's former communications chief, was recruited to help Hillary become "authentic." Schake had softened Michelle's ballsy image by having her "mom dance" with Jimmy Fallon on TV, plant a White House vegetable garden, and schlep around a Target store in suburban Alexandria, Virginia.

It was unclear how Schake intended to rehabilitate Hillary, who posed a far greater public-relations challenge than Michelle had. Clinton insiders said that Schake might send Hillary to a shopping mall, and might even have Hillary appear on the Food Network. It seemed unlikely, however, that Schake would ask Hillary to follow in Michelle's footsteps and break it down in hip-hop style.

But then, you never knew.

Schake must have remembered that, back in 1998, at the height of the Paula Jones sexual harassment suit against Bill Clinton, Hillary agreed to be photographed in a bathing suit on the beach in Saint Thomas, slow dancing with her horndog husband.

In any case, turning Hillary into a loveable Everywoman "who cares about people like me" wasn't going to be easy.

As the *New Yorker*'s Elizabeth Kolbert wrote about Hillary: "A reputation for disingenuousness would seem to be particularly damaging, since any attempt to dislodge it is bound to be construed as another piece of insincerity."

Hillary was as skeptical of the rebranding campaign as she had been of the Spielberg likeability lessons. She told friends that they reminded her of the numerous efforts that had been tried in the past—and that had failed—to make her warm and fuzzy.

"That," she said, "isn't me."

CHAPTER 15

WOULDA, COULDA, SHOULDA

> *I asked Hillary why she had chosen Yale Law School over Harvard. She laughed and said, "Harvard didn't want me."...She explained that...[a Harvard] professor looked at her and said, "We have about as many women as we need here. You should go to Yale. The teaching there is more suited to women...."*
> *...I told Hillary...I would have urged her to come to Harvard. She laughed, turned to her husband, and said, "But then I wouldn't have met him...and he wouldn't have become President."*
> **—Alan Dershowitz, Taking the Stand**

O n March 8, 2015, Bill Plante, CBS News senior White House correspondent, asked Barack Obama a direct question: When did he first learn that Hillary Clinton had used a private e-mail address, rather than the government system, while she served as his secretary of state?

"The same time everybody else learned it, through news reports," the president replied.

That was the same answer Obama had given on numerous other occasions when something went haywire on his watch.

Back in 2009, an Air Force One plane made an unauthorized photo-op pass over the Statue of Liberty. When did Obama learn about it?

"*We found out about, uh, along with all of you,*" he said.

The Fast and Furious gun-running operation in Mexico?

"*I heard on the news,*" he said.

General David Petraeus's sex scandal?

Same way.

The IRS decision to target conservative political groups?

Same.

The Justice Department's seizure of AP News reporters' phone records?

Ditto.

The National Security Agency's spying operation on friendly foreign leaders?

Ditto.

The Veterans Affairs scandal?

Ditto.

According to Obama, no one ever bothered to tell him what was up. He was in the dark, out of the loop, clueless. The buck didn't stop at his desk.

Or... there was another explanation.

He wasn't telling the truth.

That was certainly the case in the matter of Hillary's e-mails, as I learned exclusively in the course of researching this book.

"The White House explicitly warned Hillary early on in her tenure that using her private e-mail account for government business was problematic and possibly illegal," said a source who discussed the e-mail controversy with Valerie Jarrett. "People in the White House knew what Hillary was doing, because they saw her e-mails daily. Including the president. But she ignored their warnings.

"When the *New York Times* broke the story about Hillary's e-mails, the Obamas were very happy," this source continued. "Gleeful really. As far as they're concerned, Hillary and Bill brought this on themselves through sheer hubris. Valerie told me, 'The Clintons act like they're living in another century where everybody turns a blind eye. But they don't anymore.'"

Indeed, the story of Hillary's use of a private e-mail server did not come as a surprise to those who had followed her history of subterfuge and deception.

The story revived memories of past Clinton cover-ups: Whitewater, Chinagate, Travelgate, Hillary's lost billing records, the Vince Foster mystery, Filegate, Bill's perjury during the Monica Lewinsky scandal, Pardongate, the looting of White House furniture.

It exhumed the old storyline about Hillary's lack of honesty and trustworthiness and raised fresh doubts among prospective voters and deep-pocketed liberal donors, who wondered if they were backing the wrong horse in 2016.

It kindled the hopes of Hillary's potential Democratic rivals—Martin O'Malley, Joe Biden, Lincoln Chafee, Jim Webb, Bernie Sanders, and perhaps even the darkest of dark horses—Bill de Blasio and John Kerry.

And it gave fresh insight into the blood feud—both personal and political—between the Clintons and the Obamas.

When Valerie Jarrett was asked by a Bloomberg reporter if Obama had received e-mails from Hillary, she left Hillary to twist in the wind.

"That I don't know," she said. "I do know, obviously that President Obama has a very firm policy that emails should be kept on government systems. He believes in transparency."

—

Jarrett was not being truthful about what President Obama knew and when he knew it.

Back in 2012, a few months before the end of Hillary's term as secretary of state, Jarrett had summoned her to the White House to read her the riot act on a whole range of issues that the president found vexing—the Clinton Foundation's acceptance of foreign donations, Hillary's use of a private e-mail server, and Hillary's relationship with Sidney Blumenthal, a longtime Clinton fixer and undercover agent.

According to Jarrett's later recollection, which she shared with a close associate, she told Hillary that Obama considered Blumenthal to be a "thug." During the 2008 primary campaign, Blumenthal leaked malicious stories to the press that accused Obama of being a drug-using Marxist with a hidden sex life. As a result, the victorious incoming Obama administration had barred Blumenthal from working for Hillary in the State Department.

Now, Jarrett said, pacing the floor of her office and lecturing Hillary as though she were a schoolgirl, it had come to the president's attention that Hillary had ignored his directive and was in frequent contact with Blumenthal. That was unacceptable. Hillary had to cut off all communications with Blumenthal immediately.

Hillary sat stock still, staring out the window and not saying anything.

Jarrett then moved on to the next subject—Hillary's use of a private e-mail account. This was not the first time the issue had come up, Jarrett reminded Hillary. Four years ago, when Hillary first arrived at the State Department, she had been specifically warned about the security ramifications of using a private e-mail account. At the time, Jarrett went on, Hillary had given her word that she would end the use of private e-mails and instead use the authorized government account.

And yet, just the other day, the president had received an e-mail from Hillary's private account. He was furious and wanted to know why his orders had been ignored.

According to Jarrett's account of the meeting, Hillary acted bemused but made no excuses and didn't apologize.

Jarrett then raised the issue of foreign donations to the Clinton Foundation. Here was an example, she said, of something Hillary had explicitly promised in writing not to do, and was doing anyway. Hillary had struck a solemn agreement with the president. Didn't she take the president of the United States seriously?

At that, Hillary stood up and said, "This conversation is going nowhere. This meeting is over."

And she turned her back on Jarrett and walked out of the office.

In the early spring of 2015, shortly after the *Times* broke the story about Hillary's use of a private e-mail account, someone found an old ABC *20/20* report that had been available on You-Tube for the past several years and that explained why Hillary had gone to such trouble to conceal her State Department e-mails.

"As much as I've been investigated and all of that, you know," Hillary said on the video, "why would I—I don't even want—why would I ever want to do e-mail?"

In a deliberate effort at concealment, Hillary had violated State Department rules by using a private e-mail account that was linked to a server at her home in suburban Chappaqua. Under departmental rules, employees could only use private e-mails for official business if they immediately turned them over to the government to be archived.

Hillary did nothing of the sort.

She held on to her private e-mails for six years—four years as secretary of state and two more years after she left the State Department.

Hillary had to know she was in violation of the department's rules, since the State Department's inspector general had criticized one of her own ambassadors for doing the same thing.

"It is the department's general policy that normal day-to-day operations be conducted on an authorized information system, which has the proper level of security controls," the inspector general wrote about a rule that was put on the books four years before Hillary arrived at Foggy Bottom.

"Based upon my first-hand involvement in a number of things during the Clinton administration, I have absolutely no doubt that Secretary Clinton well knows the operation of the Freedom of Information Act and knows what, frankly, what she was doing," said Dan Metcalfe, who oversaw the implementation of the Freedom of Information Act at the Department of Justice. "There is no doubt in my mind and in the minds, frankly, of people at the National Archives and Records Administration, what she did was contrary to the Federal Records Act."

"Her admitted destruction of more than 30,000 emails sure looks like obstruction of justice—a serious violation of the criminal law," wrote Ronald D. Rotunda, who was assistant majority counsel to the Senate Watergate Committee. "Mrs. Clinton should know about obstruction [of justice]: Congress enacted section 1519, making the crime easier to prove, in 2002, as part of the Sarbanes-Oxley Act. As senator, she voted for the law."

━━━

The media's demand for a full accounting by Hillary opened the floodgates of criticism. But she let days go by and failed to come forward with an explanation.

"Lack of speed kills in this case," warned David Axelrod, the architect of Barack Obama's 2008 White House victory. "However this [e-mail scandal] turns out, this problem is being exacerbated by the lack of answers from the Clinton campaign . . . and it would be good to get out there and answer these questions."

But Hillary hadn't given a political press conference (as opposed to a foreign policy press conference) in more than seven years, and her handlers were afraid she was rusty. They worried she'd say something that would get her into even hotter water. She was stiff from lack of practice, they said, forgetting that Hillary had never mastered the rope-a-dope of a live political press conference.

So she delayed and delayed.

Her silence only fed the most alarming suspicions.

Had Hillary's use of a private e-mail account jeopardized national security?

Did hdr22@clintonemail.com have the same level of security employed by the government's e-mail system?

How did she know that her e-mail server hadn't been hacked?

Finally, Hillary caved under the overwhelming pressure and agreed to meet the press.

Dressed in a gray coat dress that looked a size too big for her, she emerged from a meeting at the United Nations, walked down a long hall past a copy of *Guernica*, Picasso's unsparing black, white, and gray masterpiece, and took up a position in front of twenty-five TV cameras. She looked nervous, defensive, and annoyed, as though this was the last place in the world she wanted to be. She had a hard time meeting the eyes of individual reporters, fifty of whom were gathered in a scrum behind a rope.

Reading stiffly from a prepared text, she explained that she hadn't followed the rules governing State Department e-mails, because it wasn't *convenient* to carry two phones.

In retrospect, she admitted, she woulda, coulda, shoulda.

Her explanation was laughable.

Even the most tech-challenged senior citizen knew you could have two or more e-mail accounts on one phone.

And anyway, Hillary didn't have to lug her phone around.

Huma did that for her.

But that wasn't the worst of it.

At one point during the press conference, Hillary said that she had deleted half of her e-mails—about thirty thousand of them—because they were "personal" and concerned things like her yoga appointments and preparations for Chelsea's wedding. At another point, she contradicted herself and said that those "personal" e-mails remained on a private server at her home in Chappaqua.

Trust me, she said, *my lawyers have carefully combed through each of the sixty thousand or so e-mails and sent the work-related ones—about thirty thousand—to the State Department.*

But her lawyers never reviewed each e-mail.

According to *Time* magazine, the legal "review did not involve opening and reading each email; instead, Clinton's lawyers created a list of names and keywords related to her work and searched for those."

As the *Atlantic* put it: "The idea that such a process could produce 'absolute confidence' that all public records were identified is as curious as the notion that Bill Clinton never inhaled."

By the end of her press conference, Hillary looked guiltier than when she started it. What's more, in the following days and weeks, the public learned even more disquieting news. Hillary had ordered her aides to wipe her hard drive clean, thereby destroying the thirty thousand so-called "personal" e-mails on her private server.

By any measure, it was a massive political cover-up, second only to the most famous case of evidence tampering on behalf of a high-ranking official of the U.S. government—the eighteen-and-a-half-minute gap in the Nixon tapes.

———

Hillary's twenty-one-minute press conference was almost universally deemed a failure.

"When Hillary first approached the podium," wrote Ashe Schow, a staff writer at the *Washington Examiner*, "she was all smiles and held her head high; she looked at ease. 'Look at all the little people come to see me,' her demeanor seemed to suggest. She rattled off some information about the Clinton Foundation's latest report detailing the problems women face worldwide. She took a shot at Republicans for sending a letter to Iran. She then read from her prepared remarks addressing her ongoing email scandal.

"But as the questions kept coming and moved beyond those that simply allowed her to reiterate her prepared remarks, Clinton became visibly irritated," Schow continued. "Her answers were shorter and she began talking over reporters. Finally, a woman touched her arm and it was time to end the event.

"If she expected the mainstream media to take her press conference as a signal to end the unflattering story, she was wrong."

Indeed, John F. Harris, the editor in chief of *Politico*, spoke for most of the mainstream press when he wrote that beneath Hillary's politesse "was an unmistakable message [to the media]...easily distilled into three short words: Go to hell."

Rem Rieder, editor at large and media columnist for *USA Today*, agreed: "Clinton put on a clinic on how not to defuse a crisis.... But even worse than the substance [of what she said] was the manner. Clinton seemed imperial, rigid, above it all—and too clever by half. As the ordeal dragged on, her body language made clear she'd rather be anywhere else in the world rather than batting down these questions from these wretched reporters....

"Candidates need to undergo this intense scrutiny not for the special interests of news outlets but for the American people. This is a big, important job these candidates are applying for.

"And if Clinton finds this experience unendurable, maybe she should be applying for a different job."

CHAPTER 16

"SKIN IN THE GAME"

The president shared his account of the Lewinsky matter with me. . . . He did so unguardedly and freely, under the assumption that we were speaking in complete privacy. What I told the grand jury under oath supports completely what the president has told the American people and is contrary to any charge that the president has done anything wrong.
—*Sidney Blumenthal, June 25, 1998*

Several years ago, I wrote a book called *The Kennedy Curse*, which examined how tragedy haunted one of America's most powerful families.

Hillary Clinton reminded me of the Kennedys in one notable way.

Hubris led members of the Kennedy family to take risks that often ended in calamity and death. In Hillary's case, hubris led to a different kind of self-destruction. When presented with the choice of doing the right thing or doing the wrong thing, she compulsively chose the unethical alternative and ended up mired in scandal and disgrace.

A perfect example of how Hillary constantly chose the unethical alternative was a letter she sent to Representative Trey Gowdy, the Republican chairman of the House Select Committee investigating the deadly terrorist attacks in Benghazi. In her letter, Hillary insisted that the only private e-mail address she ever used while secretary of state was hdr22@clintonemail.com.

That was a lie.

In fact, she had used a second secret e-mail address, HRod17@clintonemail.com, and didn't tell Gowdy about it.

She had kept this e-mail address secret because it had been used in subterranean exchanges with Sidney Blumenthal, who was acting as her secret back channel on Libya.

There were several problems with this cozy arrangement. At the same time that he was advising Hillary, Blumenthal was on the payrolls of the rabid left-wing website Media Matters and the liberal super PAC American Bridge. What's more, he was being paid $10,000 a month by the Clinton Foundation.

In addition, Blumenthal worked for two companies seeking contracts in Libya. As the *New York Times* noted: "Blumenthal said that Libya's prime minister was bringing in new economic advisers, and that a businessman, Najib Obeida, was among 'the most influential of this group.' At the time, Mr. Obeida was a potential business partner of a group of contractors whom Mr. Blumenthal was advising."

"The *New York Times* story on Sidney Blumenthal perfectly encapsulates everything wrong with the Clinton operation," wrote Rich Lowry, the editor of *National Review*. "Blumenthal is banned from the State Department by discerning Obama aides, so he works for the Clinton Foundation—on nebulous 'message guidance,' among other things—while whispering in Hillary's ear about Libya, at the same time he's working with business interests hoping to make money in Libya on projects that would have required State Department permits. This is how a charity is supposed to work?"

—

If you could pan an imaginary iPhone camera across the trajectory of Hillary's long career—from Little Rock to the White House to the Senate to her first race for the White House to the State Department to her second race for the White House—you would detect a clear pattern of behavior: she repeated the same transgressions over and over again. For her, the drive for power, success, and money always overrode standards of honor and decency.

As a result, she stained her record as secretary of state with so many scandals that it was hard to keep them straight.

Here are some of her most egregious offenses.

THE BENGHAZI CONNECTION

Hillary lied when she said that officials "at the assistant secretary level or below" had failed to keep her informed about requests for beefed-up security at the U.S. outpost in Benghazi. In *Blood Feud: The Clintons vs. the Obamas*, I reported that in the months leading up to the attack on the U.S. mission, Cheryl Mills and Jake Sullivan, among others, made Hillary aware that the mission was highly vulnerable to assault from bands of heavily armed Islamic militiamen roaming the streets of Benghazi.

I also wrote in *Blood Feud* that Hillary knowingly lied when she said that the attack on America's diplomatic compound in Benghazi was in response to an inflammatory video posted on the Internet. Hillary's false statement about the video was proof she was willing to go to any length to prevent Benghazi from becoming a political embarrassment to the White House and the State Department.

Confirmation of what I reported came in May 2015—a year after *Blood Feud* was published—when the State Department released nearly nine hundred pages of Hillary's e-mails.

Among other things, the e-mails proved that Hillary's top aides had in fact warned her about the dangerous security conditions in Benghazi. A year and a half *before* the attack, Huma Abedin sent Hillary an e-mail noting that Ambassador Christopher Stevens, who would lose his life in the attack, was scheduled to meet the Libyan foreign minister to make "a written request for better security at the hotel [in Benghazi] and for better security-related coordination." And Elizabeth Dibble, the deputy secretary in the Bureau of Near Eastern Affairs, e-mailed Hillary that "State of Embassy Tripoli facility:...the facility is not salvageable—the condition is 'shocking and photos don't do it justice.'"

As for who was behind the attack, Sidney Blumenthal e-mailed Hillary two days after the assault that "sensitive sources" had confirmed that the attack was orchestrated by Ansar al-Sharia, an al Qaeda affiliate.

The nine hundred released e-mails showed that Hillary covered up the role of terrorism in the attack because Barack Obama, seeking a second term as president, didn't want to admit that al Qaeda was still a major threat. When the false narrative about a "spontaneous" protest would no longer wash, Hillary's deputy, Jake Sullivan, assured Hillary that she was off the hook. "Attached is full compilation [of your public statements on Benghazi]," Sullivan e-mailed Hillary. "You never said spontaneous or characterized the motives. In fact you were careful in your first statement to say we were just assessing motive and method."

Of course, that wasn't true either.

THE ELECTRIC-CAR CONNECTION

While Hillary was secretary of state, her younger brother Tony Rodham received special favors from the U.S. government for a company owned by an old Clinton crony named Terry McAuliffe.

In case you've forgotten, Tony Rodham was the brother who received a "consultant's fee" to arrange an eleventh-hour presidential pardon from President Bill Clinton for a married couple serving time for bank fraud.

As for McAuliffe, he once sat on the board of the Clinton Foundation and liked to describe himself as the "Godzilla" of Democratic fund-raising. McAuliffe was the pal who pledged $1.35 million in cash to secure a mortgage for the Clintons when they left the White House "dead broke." The Clintons returned the favor. McAuliffe won the governor's race in Virginia in 2014 with considerable help from Bill and Hillary, who campaigned by his side and donated $100,000 to his race.

You didn't get closer to the Clintons than that.

Unless, of course, you were a blood relative like Tony Rodham.

According to a report by the inspector general for the Department of Homeland Security, a top U.S. official gave an "unprecedented" level of special treatment to GreenTech Automotive, where Tony worked as a $72,000-a-year "facilitator" raising money from wealthy investors.

McAuliffe sought Tony Rodham's help in getting special visas from the Department of Homeland Security for foreigners who promised to invest $550,000 or more in his electric car company.

And Hillary's bro was only too happy to oblige.

He used his influence to obtain the visas.

THE HAITI CONNECTION

While his sister was secretary of state, Tony Rodham was appointed to the advisory board of VCS Mining, a U.S.-based company that received a gold-mining contract in Haiti.

It just so happened that Bill Clinton was the UN special envoy to Haiti; he was known on the island nation, only half-jokingly, as "the governor of Haiti." As for Secretary of State Hillary Clinton, she had a decisive say over America's multimillion-dollar relief efforts in that earthquake-ravaged country. In short, the Clintons influenced where the money went in Haiti and who got the bankable jobs.

"The two agencies in the world that can run these [relief operations] are the United States and the United Nations, and the Clintons sit atop this package," said former senator Tim Wirth, president of the UN Foundation.

And where did Tony Rodham meet the chief executive of VCS Mining, the company that owned the Haitian gold mine?

At a meeting of the Clinton Global Initiative, natch.

And Tony Rodham's Haitian connection didn't stop there. He was also involved in a failed $22 million deal to build homes in Haiti.

"I deal through the Clinton Foundation," Tony explained. "That gets me in touch with the Haitian officials. I hound my brother-in-law, because it's his fund that we're going to get our money from."

THE NIGERIAN CONNECTION

While Hillary was secretary of state, she refused time after time to designate the al Qaeda–linked Nigerian Islamist group Boko Haram as a terrorist organization. Hillary's stance on the issue bewildered human-rights groups, since Boko Haram had earned an international reputation for its brutal kidnappings and enslavement of Nigerian schoolgirls, and Hillary had made protecting women and children a central issue of her term as secretary of state.

When Senator David Vitter, Louisiana Republican, looked into the matter, he discovered an intriguing connection between Hillary and a shadowy Lebanese-Nigerian billionaire named

Gilbert Chagoury, who had given millions of dollars to the Clinton Foundation and was one of its biggest donors.

A one-time adviser to Sani Abacha, Nigeria's late and unlamented dictator, Chagoury owned one of the largest construction conglomerates in Nigeria. *Investor's Business Daily* reported that Chagoury had a financial interest in keeping Boko Haram off the list of worldwide terrorist organizations.

Senator Vitter agreed.

"He's not Boko Haram," Vitter said of Chagoury, "but he has a clear interest in terms of his commercial developments of not getting this [terrorist] designation, which would put the brakes on a lot of possible development that he wants in Nigeria."

As long as Hillary was at Foggy Bottom, the murderous Boko Haram stayed off the terror list.

THE CANADIAN CONNECTION

While Hillary was secretary of state, she reviewed a pending free-trade agreement with Colombia. It wasn't the first time she had grappled with this issue. When she ran for president in 2008, Hillary had opposed the trade deal because of Colombia's poor record on workers' rights.

This time, however, the stakes were different. The deal affected a company founded by a rich Canadian mining financier named Frank Giustra, who was Bill Clinton's close buddy and who had donated millions to the Clinton Foundation.

According to Peter Schweizer, the author of *Clinton Cash*, Giustra made his private jet available to Bill when the former president traveled to South America to deliver a speech. In return for the favor, Bill arranged a meeting between Giustra and Colombian president Alvaro Uribe to help Giustra develop his business in that country.

Not surprisingly, Hillary dropped her hostility to the trade deal and gave it her stamp of approval, allowing Giustra to reap huge profits.

That wasn't the only instance in which Hillary smoothed the skids for Frank Giustra while she was secretary of state. Along with several other rich investors, Giustra wanted to sell a Canadian mining company to Rosatom, the Russian atomic energy agency. The sale required approval from the State Department and several other agencies of the U.S. government, for if the deal went through, it would give Vladimir Putin control over 20 percent of the uranium production capacity in the United States.

Given Giustra's connection to Bill and the Clinton Foundation, Hillary should have recused herself in the matter. Instead, she voted in favor of letting the sale go through.

"As the Russians gradually assumed control of Uranium One in three separate transactions from 2009 to 2013, Canadian records show, a flow of cash made its way to the Clinton Foundation," the *New York Times* reported in a lengthy front-page story that jumped inside the paper and continued for two full pages.

"Uranium One's chairman [Frank Giustra] used his family foundation to make four donations totaling $2.5 million," the story continued. "Those contributions were not publicly disclosed by the Clintons.... And shortly after the Russians announced their intention to acquire a majority stake in Uranium One, Mr. Clinton received $500,000 for a Moscow speech from a Russian investment bank with links to the Kremlin that was promoting Uranium One stock."

Bill Clinton made almost $48 million in speaking fees while his wife was secretary of state.

As for Frank Giustra, he denied any wrongdoing. He pointed out that he was just one of 1,100 *undisclosed* donors to the Clinton Foundation, most of them foreigners. The donations were routed through the Clinton Giustra Enterprise Partnership in Canada, which bundled the money and sent it along to the Clinton Foundation in America.

Oops! Giustra had spilled the beans about the foundation's failure to disclose the names of its foreign donors. The news was a political bombshell, for as a condition of becoming secretary of state, Hillary had promised Obama that the foundation would disclose *all* of its donors.

Worse yet, Giustra made the foundation sound like an international money-laundering scheme.

"Rather than taking cash from blatantly illegal activities (as far as we know) and then cleaning it up by running it through legitimate businesses before it ends up at its final destination," wrote the Federalist's Sean Davis, "the Clinton Foundation mops up cash from wealthy foreigners, bundles it within a larger organization to hide the money's original source, and then funnels the cash from that legitimate charity right into the Clinton Foundation coffers."

The Charity Navigator, a nonprofit watchdog, apparently agreed. It put the Clinton Foundation on its "watch list" along with Al Sharpton's National Action Network.

"I wonder if any aspirant for the presidency except Hillary Clinton could survive such a [documented series of scandals]," Peggy Noonan wrote. "I suspect she can because the Clintons are unique in the annals of American politics: They are protected from charges of corruption by their reputation for corruption. It's not news anymore."

THE QATAR CONNECTION

While Hillary was secretary of state, soccer's top governing body, the Fédération Internationale de Football Association (FIFA), awarded Qatar, a tiny oil-rich Arab state with a population of just two million people, the lucrative rights to host the World Cup in 2022.

Qatar was, to say the least, a puzzling choice. Among its many drawbacks, the desert kingdom had a terrible record of human-rights abuses, no soccer history, and summer temperatures that reached 122 degrees Fahrenheit, which made it too hot to play soccer.

Rumors had been circulating for years that the World Cup bidding process wasn't kosher. It was suspected that the votes of some of FIFA's officials were for sale to the highest bidder. And indeed, in May 2015, several of those officials were arrested in Zurich, Switzerland, and charged with a massive corruption scheme, including racketeering, wire fraud, and money laundering. The U.S. Department of Justice charged that the officials had enriched themselves to the tune of $150 million.

At the time Qatar won the World Cup bid, Bill Clinton was an honorary chairman of the committee that put together the

U.S. bid. Shortly after Bill's committee lost its bid, the United States, along with Australia, hired private investigators to look into the bidding process.

Qatar's winning committee suddenly ponied up between $250,000 and $500,000 to the Clinton Foundation in an effort, as the Daily Beast put it, to "make it up" to Bill. That sum was on top of the $1 million to $5 million that the state of Qatar had already given the foundation.

While all this was going on, the United States was negotiating an $11 billion arms sale to Qatar that was approved shortly after Hillary left the State Department.

THE UBS CONNECTION

While she was secretary of state, Hillary took the highly questionable step of intervening to fix a problem that UBS, a giant of the Swiss banking industry, was having with the IRS. The story of Hillary's dodgy behavior was broken by Kimberley A. Strassel, a member of the *Wall Street Journal*'s editorial board, who writes a weekly column for the *Journal* titled "Potomac Watch."

"In the years that followed [Hillary's intervention on behalf of UBS]," Strassel wrote, "UBS donated $600,000 to the Clinton Foundation, anted up another $32 million in loans via foundation programs, and dropped $1.5 million on Bill for a series of speaking events. Both sides deny any quid pro quo. But the pattern is clear: More than 60 major firms that lobbied the State Department during Mrs. Clinton's tenure also donated some $26 million to her family's foundation."

—

"It never seems to end," wrote Tom Bevan, the cofounder and executive editor of RealClearPolitics. "Drip, drip, drip. The web of global and corporate connections to the Clinton Foundation is so vast, there's virtually no issue on which Hillary Clinton can comment without her being immediately tied, via foundation donations or her or her husband's paid speaking engagements, to some entity with skin in the game."

CHAPTER 17

A "CLASSIC WASHINGTON OMELETTE"

*He who permits himself to tell a lie once finds it much
easier to do it a second and third time, till at length it
becomes habitual. He tells lies without attending to
it, and truths without the world's believing him. This
falsehood of the tongue leads to that of the heart, and in
time depraves all its good dispositions.*
—*Thomas Jefferson*

In the past, Hillary had always managed to wriggle out of
tight places, and many of her supporters on the Left were
rooting for her to pull off another Houdini act.

Her followers had good reason to believe Hillary would
succeed. After all, the Clintons were past masters at weathering
scandals, from the trivial (revelations that the Clintons took a tax
deduction on Bill's donated underwear) to the consequential (an
impeachment trial for lying under oath about Bill's sexual relationship with Monica Lewinsky).

"The Clintons have been sent off to their certain doom more
times than Tyrion Lannister," wrote Matt Latimer, a former
speechwriter for President George W. Bush. "Yet whatever the

storm—from blue dresses to funny money from China to an actual impeachment trial—Bill and Hillary are this generation's Six-Million Dollar Man (and Woman). They always rebuild faster, stronger, and a hell of a lot richer than ever."

The Clintons' battle-tested strategy was simple: wait out the first wave of attacks, then step forward and say there's nothing new.

"Republicans trying to turn the Benghazi attacks into a scandal that taints Hillary Clinton's chances at a 2016 presidential run must realize that scandals don't weaken Hillary Clinton," left-wing scourge Bill Maher sounded off on his cable TV show. "They only make her stronger. Travelgate, the Rose Law Firm, Whitewater, Vince Foster, Monica Lewinsky.... Hillary eats scandals for breakfast."

But this time it appeared that the scandals might be consuming Hillary, rather than the other way around.

Because this time was different.

During Hillary's previous scandals, she had not occupied a public office. "Co-president" was a nickname, not an official title. As secretary of state, however, she had been confirmed by the U.S. Senate. She held a great public trust. She was the face of America around the world, the first among equals in the president's cabinet, and the fourth in the presidential line of succession.

And now she was asking Americans to *trust* her and *elect* her as their president.

"Hillary Clinton," wrote Michael Barone, author of *The Almanac of American Politics*, "is in a different position. She is a candidate...and candidates are easily dispensed with, as former

Senator Gary Hart learned when the photos of him sailing on the 'Monkey Business' appeared in May 1987 when he was seeking the Democratic nomination for president. His staffers vowed he would hold onto his support, but it wasn't his to hold on to. He quickly withdrew and faded from view."

Turning a $1,000 bet on cattle futures into $100,000 when you were the first lady of Arkansas was one thing; turning the office of the U.S. secretary of state into a money machine for your husband, your relatives, and your family's foundation was something else.

If you believed the polls, Hillary's cheating and chicanery were beginning to erode her reputation among potential voters. According to a Quinnipiac poll that was conducted in the spring of 2015, 61 percent of independent voters—the voters she needed to win the White House—did not think Hillary was honest.

A month later, Quinnipiac did a poll of Democratic voters and came up with pretty much the same result: a majority—53 percent—did not feel that Hillary was "honest and trustworthy."

Yet another poll, this one conducted by the Associated Press and GfK, one of the world's largest marketing research organizations, found that a majority of people did not find Hillary inspiring and likeable.

And the rapid drop in Hillary's "favorability" ratings continued throughout the summer months and into the fall, dimming her prospects of capturing the White House.

For instance, another Quinnipiac University poll found that Hillary would lose Colorado by nine points in a matchup against Wisconsin governor Scott Walker, and that she would lose Iowa by at least six points to Walker, former Florida governor Jeb Bush, and Senator Marco Rubio.

When voters were asked if Hillary "cares about the needs and problems of people like you or not," 57 percent of respondents in Colorado replied that she did not.

In late July, Niall Stanage, associate editor of the political paper the *Hill*, published a story about the mounting fear among Democratic insiders that Hillary was a deeply flawed candidate who could lose to a Republican challenger in 2016. And Charlie Cook, the highly respected political analyst and editor and publisher of *The Cook Political Report*, wrote a piece for *National Journal* titled "Is Clinton's Tide Shifting?"

"Up until now," Cook wrote, "the controversy regarding then-Secretary of State Hillary Clinton's private email server has been one that has consumed only those who fit into one or more of the following categories: conservative Republicans, regular Fox News–watchers, conservative talk-radio listeners, or Clinton-haters (both professional and amateur)....

"The most recent development—that the inspector general of the intelligence community found that in a sample of 40 e-mails provided by Clinton from her server, four (or 10 percent) included classified material—potentially puts a different twist on things.... this story would seem to reinforce critics' claims that the Clintons don't play by the rules."

Going one step further, Gabriel Schoenfeld, a senior fellow at the Hudson Institute in Washington, D.C., asserted: "The bad news for Team Hillary is that this issue [using her private e-mail server for classified material] is going to fester. Indeed, over the next months, given the law, precedent and facts already on the record, the imbroglio holds the potential to kill her candidacy."

◼

"We...see a pattern of financial transactions involving the Clintons that occurred contemporaneous with favorable U.S. policy decisions benefiting those providing the funds," Peter Schweizer noted. "During Hillary's years of public service, the Clintons have conducted or facilitated hundreds of large transactions [with foreigners]. Some of these transactions have put millions in their own pockets."

Skeptics raised an objection.

They said the evidence of wrongdoing by Hillary was purely circumstantial; no one had produced proof that she had provided favors in return for speaking fees or donations to the Clinton Foundation.

"It is highly unlikely that very much of what Schweizer alleges will stick, if only because that classic Washington omelette made of equal parts policy and political reasons can never be unmade once it's cooked," wrote one of the skeptics, Michael Hirsh. "Especially among the uber-cautious Clintons, you'll never find the smoking ingredient; no one will ever be caught saying, 'Let's make a policy decision for Bill's donors.'"

The skeptics demanded a smoking gun.

They were demanding hard evidence.

Something on paper.

Like a document or a sworn affidavit or...an e-mail.

But Hillary had wiped her private e-mail server clean. She had destroyed half of all her e-mail communications while she was secretary of state.

She had made it all but impossible to find a smoking gun.

Or had she?

CHAPTER 18

THE SMOLDERING GUN?

The smoking gun. Whoo! That sounded dramatic.
—*Raymond "Red" Reddington in the NBC series* The Blacklist

Even the most partisan skeptics on the Left agreed that Hillary's chances of becoming president would be radically reduced if a smoking gun could be found.

But what constituted a smoking gun?

And what if the only thing that could be found was a *smoldering* gun?

In an attempt to answer those questions, in this chapter I offer interviews with three people who had firsthand knowledge of Hillary's involvement with the Clinton Foundation while she was secretary of state.

Each of these people spoke on the condition of anonymity. But as witnesses, they corroborate each other's stories.

INTERVIEW ONE

"I worked for Hillary and saw a lot of what was going on," a college student who interned at Foggy Bottom during Hillary's last year there said in an interview for this book. "One of my jobs was to go into the conference room that's adjacent to the secretary's office and gather up papers that were used by Hillary, Cheryl, Huma, and others during their meetings. It was like I was the invisible man. Nobody gave me a second look. They obviously didn't think it mattered what a young intern saw, so they didn't make an effort to hide anything from me.

"The Clinton Foundation and the Clinton Global Initiative have very distinct logos," the intern continued. "The foundation's logo is an open circle of stars surrounding the words Clinton Foundation. The Global Initiative's logo is similar, but the stars are gold and they're intersected by four curved lines like parenthesis marks. Often, when I went into the secretary of state's conference room, I saw those logos on papers that were strewn all over the big table.

"While I was organizing the papers into neat piles, I couldn't resist taking a look. They were fund-raising papers with the names and dates of contacts on them. There was no mistaking the fact that Hillary and her closest advisers at State were working on foundation and Global Initiative business.

"I mostly recall snippets of conversation that I overheard when I delivered papers from the conference room to Huma and Cheryl and to Hillary's secretaries.

"I remember one time when Hillary came back from Russia. It must have been the fall of 2012, toward the end of her run at

State, and Hillary came into the office wearing one of those Russian fur hats. That was the day I overheard her talking on her cell phone, discussing a contribution to the foundation from a Russian guy. I knew he was Russian because she turned to Huma and said, 'The fucking translator is so goddamn slow with the Russian.'

"Another time, I delivered a bunch of papers to Cheryl, who was waiting for them in Hillary's office. The papers were for Hillary to initial and sign. Hillary was in a really crappy mood that day. It looked to me like she was conducting several phone calls on different phones at the same time. The one thing I heard her say was, 'Bill, I won't do that. I won't say that. *You* tell the president you don't want to see him, if that's how you feel.'

"I was shocked. Here I was, in the secretary's inner office, overhearing her talk to the former president, and I shouldn't have been there, and for a moment I was so scared I couldn't move my legs.

"Huma came in and saw me and shoved me toward the door. And the last thing I heard was Hillary saying, 'Oh, fuck off, Bill!' and then she threw the cell phone on the floor and it bounced off the rug."

INTERVIEW TWO

"During her last year at the State Department, Hillary's priorities took on a different character," a Foreign Service officer with more than two decades of experience said in an interview. "In 2012, her priorities were first, raising money for her presidential run; second, raising money for the Clinton Foundation; and third, tending to the business of foreign policy.

"She obviously had a busy schedule and had to meet with foreign ministers and other dignitaries, but those meetings seemed rushed and pro forma," the diplomat continued. "Her real passions were the Clinton Foundation and talking to political strategists like John Podesta, James Carville, Paul Begala, and others. She met in her seventh-floor office with political bundlers, and she had long conversations on strategy with Bill.

"In my time at State, I never saw a secretary so disconnected from her job. She seemed to consider the running of U.S. foreign policy a side job. She was focused on getting the *big* job—the White House. Everything was about keeping information about her campaign plans from leaking back to the Obama White House. She didn't trust anybody but her small inner circle. She was completely paranoid, whispering, covering her mouth in case somebody could read lips."

INTERVIEW THREE

"When she flew on her Air Force C-32," said another veteran Foreign Service officer, "Hillary took along stacks of papers in manila folders that were marked 'CF' and 'CGO'—the Clinton Foundation and the Clinton Global initiative. They had dividers labeled 'Donations,' 'Fund Raising,' 'AIDS/HIV,' 'Haiti,' and so forth.

"She didn't try to cover up her involvement with the foundation," this person continued. "One time, after she returned from a grueling trip to Asia that included numerous stops at various capitals, she gave a cocktail party for her staff in a room near her office. It was summertime, a hot, humid day in July, and Hillary talked about the Clinton Foundation and how well fund-raising was going for Haiti and HIV work. She talked about Bill's accomplishments in lowering the price of AIDS drugs. She was beaming with pride.

"Hillary made it clear to those of us who came within her orbit that she kept up with the work of the foundation and the Global Initiative at the same time that she ran the State Department. She said she had no qualms, because the work she did at State and the work at the foundation and the Global Initiative were related and complemented each other.

"In her mind, there was no conflict of interest. She was doing good work, solving the most daunting problems, and making the United States look like the good guy around the world. She always said her work was twice as hard because she was constantly cleaning up the messes George W. Bush left behind.

"I remember a conversation she had with Bill. I believe it was late in the summer of 2012, because the presidential election campaign was just beginning to heat up. We were on her plane, refueling at some Air Force base in Germany, and I was sitting behind her while she spoke on a phone. All I could hear was her side of the conversation. She was berating Bill. She told him that he had given her rotten advice on dealing with Putin. She should have been tougher with the Russians. She said, 'Bill, you are so up their asses your judgment sucks.'

"Then she gave him hell about having his picture taken with two hookers. The photos were circulating all over the Internet, and it made him look like a laughingstock for the umpteenth time. There was a long silence while she listened to him, and then all of a sudden she said, 'Bill, I am fucking hanging up! Good-bye!'"

PART V

This puzzle I've been keeping
Has been in hiding creeping out the closet door
Spilling out onto the floor
How long will I be picking up pieces
How long will I be picking up my heart
—Blue October, "Picking Up Pieces"

CHAPTER 19

THE POLITICAL ANIMAL

*What happened in 2008 was that Hillary's candidacy got
out in front of any rationale for it, and the danger is that
that's happening again.*
—David Axelrod

O ver the course of many months, Bill Clinton had been
charting a course that he believed would lead Hillary to
the White House.

He took great pride in his reputation as "the best
political animal that's ever been in American politics," as Charlie
Rose once described him. Yet in typical Bill Clinton fashion, his
grand plan for Hillary was a random collection of ideas—some
of them workable, some of them not so workable, some of them
zany, and some of them calculated to piss off Hillary.

For instance, one of his ideas called for Hillary to get rid of
her pantsuits.

He had never liked that look on her.

"Toss them all in the fireplace," he said, according to a close Clinton source.

But the more Bill complained about her pantsuits, the more Hillary was determined to wear them.

She always had a thing about men trying to force women to wear what *men* wanted. Like high heels and lingerie. It was a pet peeve since her college days.

She and Bill frequently clashed on the subject.

He made his "suggestions" about her wardrobe.

And she did the opposite.

Bill was also on Hillary's case about her looks. She couldn't do anything about the calendar—she'd be sixty-nine years old in 2016—but she could do something about the lines and sagging skin on her face. He wanted her to get a facelift.

But once again, Hillary had her own ideas.

She had no intention of going to a clinic, where she would be recognized and almost certainly photographed by someone with a smartphone. The media would jump all over the photos—and so would her political opponents.

Instead, Hillary asked a well-known New York plastic surgeon to come to her home in Chappaqua. After several consultations, she and the doctor agreed on a course of action. She cleared the house of servants and gave instructions to her Secret Service detail not to let anyone pass beyond the driveway gate. The plastic surgeon and his team then set up a mini–operating room in her home with the latest medical equipment.

"She had her cheeks lifted, and her wrinkles and lines Botoxed," said one of Hillary's friends in an interview for this book. "She had work done on her eyes as well as on her neck and forehead. She took it gradually and didn't have anything drastic done, because she wanted to evaluate the changes as she proceeded. If it had started to make her look weird, she would have stopped it immediately. It was a pretty big deal and required multiple visits. It worked out well. You can see the subtle differences in her photographs."

———

"To be really good at [politics] you've gotta like people," Bill Clinton said. "You've gotta like policy. And you've gotta like politics. You've gotta have a pain threshold. You have to understand there's a reason this is a contact sport."

Hillary wasn't good at politics because (1) she didn't like people, and (2) a lot of people—nearly half the voting-age population of America—didn't like her.

Her unlikeability manifested itself in several ways.

At the height of her book tour for *Hard Choices*, the editors of *People* put Hillary on the cover of their magazine. They expected to sell a million copies or more of the magazine; instead, the Hillary cover turned out to be *People*'s worst-selling issue of 2014.

Simon & Schuster paid Hillary a $14 million advance for *Hard Choices*. According to book industry sources, one way for the publisher to avoid taking a write-off, or "a bath," would have been for it to sell 2,700,000 hardcover copies over two years. Nielsen BookScan, which tracks about 80 percent of hardcover sales, reported that *Hard Choices* sold fewer than three hundred thousand copies. What's more, her memoir was knocked off its short-lived perch atop the *New York Times* bestseller list by my book *Blood Feud*, which compounded her humiliation.

A WMUR Granite State poll from the University of New Hampshire, which was conducted a year before that state's primary contest, showed that Hillary had started losing ground the moment she announced her candidacy; she trailed three of her potential Republican challengers—Jeb Bush, Rand Paul, and Marco Rubio. Another University of New Hampshire poll revealed that just three in ten voters thought Hillary was the most likeable of the potential Democratic candidates.

She gave the other seven voters ample reason to find her unlikeable.

Her maladroit press conference at the United Nations, in which she defended her use of private e-mails, didn't win her any converts. The consensus of opinion was that she came across as sanctimonious and hypocritical—not exactly attributes designed to win the hearts and minds of voters.

That press conference, reported *New York* magazine, "served to remind [people] of something many had forgotten: what an abominable candidate she can be."

Many political consultants to whom the author spoke agreed with that judgment. They pointed out that Hillary's two electoral victories—for a U.S. Senate seat from New York in 2000 and 2006—were earned in a solid blue state against weak and underfunded opponents, Rick Lazio and John Spencer.

When she had some real competition—from Obama in 2008—she lost.

The conservative political commentator Pat Buchanan opined that, unlike John Kennedy and Ronald Reagan, Hillary was not a natural "political athlete."

"She's like Pete Rose, who has to grind out every hit," said Buchanan.

Hillary was prone to unforced errors, as she proved with her famous whoppers.

On Benghazi: "What difference at this point does it make?"

On her sky-high speaking fees: "We came out of the White House not only dead broke but in debt."

On whether Sergeant Bowe Bergdahl deserted or was captured by the Taliban: "It doesn't matter."

On job growth: "Don't let anybody tell you that it's corporations and businesses that create jobs."

She also displayed a political tin ear.

At a Georgetown University speech, Hillary declared that Americans needed to "show respect for our enemies" and "empathize with their perspective and point of view."

During the ensuing flap over her remark, Secretary of State John Kerry explained that Hillary wasn't referring to enemies like the Islamic State, but "only" to adversaries like Russia. But Kerry, like Hillary, missed the point. Showing "respect" for Russia was what led Vladimir Putin to believe that America was in retreat; it encouraged him to invade Ukraine and annex Crimea.

It didn't help Hillary's likeability quotient when it became known that she not only demanded $250,000 to $300,000 per speech from cash-strapped universities and colleges, but she also demanded that they provide her with a spread of hummus and crudité in the green room backstage.

"Hillary still obsesses about money," wrote Maureen Dowd, "a narrative thread that has existed since she was thwarted in her desire to build a pool at the governor's mansion in poor Arkansas and left the White House with a doggie bag full of sofas, rugs, lamps, TVs and china, some of which the Clintons later had to pay for or return."

As a campaigner, said Dee Dee Myers, who served as Bill's press secretary, Hillary made the mistake of *telling* audiences what she felt rather than *showing* them.

"The presidency," said Meyers, "isn't all that powerful, except as the bully pulpit. It comes down to your ability to get people to follow you, to inspire. You have to lead. Can [Hillary] get people to come together, or does she remain such a polarizing figure?"

For an answer to that question, all you had to do was ask half the voters in the United States, who didn't like Hillary.

—

In total contrast to Hillary, Bill was brilliant at politics because (1) he liked people, (2) they liked him, and (3) he treated all politics—even presidential politics—like *local* politics.

"He'll show up at your birthday party in suburban Cleveland if he thinks you can be useful to him down the pike," said one of his closest advisers. "Can you imagine the impact that has—his showing up at a middle-class home out of nowhere? You never forget it, and you tell everybody you know about it.

"These other guys in politics don't get the power of that kind of thing," his adviser continued. "The ripple effect it has politically over the long term. Bill does. He's been doing that since he was in high school."

Bill's staff at the Clinton Library kept a massive computerized list of political operatives from the highest level to the precinct level all across the country. The list included people in solid red states, which Bill refused to cede to the Republicans. Along with their names, telephone numbers, and snail-mail and e-mail addresses were the names of their spouses and children. Bill made sure that a personal note with his signature went out on birthdays and anniversaries. And if the person who was celebrating was important enough, Bill thought nothing of getting on his plane and making a personal appearance.

There was a Yiddish word for Bill.

He was *haymish*—someone you could feel comfortable with.

And there was a Yiddish word for Hillary.

When it came to politics, she was a klutz.

CHAPTER 20

"WHEN YOU GOT IT, FLAUNT IT"

The campaigner in chief [Bill Clinton] is always more an asset than anything. He's good for money, he's good for strategy, and he's good for turnout. That's the holy trinity of good campaigning.
—*Democratic pollster Jefrey Pollock*

O ne spring night, three family friends joined Bill, Hillary, and Chelsea for dinner in Chappaqua. Afterward, they carried their glasses of Chardonnay over to Bill's home office in the red barn.

As was his custom, Bill held forth about presidential politics and campaign strategy. He enumerated the things Hillary needed to do in order to win the presidency, and he ticked off each point on his fingers as he went along. One of the guests later provided a summary of what Bill said—some in paraphrases and some in direct quotes.

First, Bill told Hillary, you must protect your left flank in the primary campaign. Feed the base red meat. Income inequality.

Prison reform. Gay marriage. Climate change. Path to citizenship for undocumented immigrants. Paid family leave. Don't worry about looking like you're running against my pro-growth legacy and me. After you get elected, you can do whatever you want.

Second, this is going to be the most expensive race in history, so it's vitally important that you control the money machine. Forget campaign-finance reform and get in bed with a super PAC. Hammer those rich guys in the penthouses and mansions. Corner the big progressive donors so they won't fund O'Malley or, God forbid, Elizabeth Warren.

"Rake in the dough as fast as possible," he said. "You don't ever want to run out of money like you did last time [in 2008]."

Third, hold on to Obama's support among blacks and Hispanics while galvanizing female voters to elect the first woman president. Women are more likely to vote than men are, and the female vote will decide the next election.

Fourth, "hire away Obama's best and brightest. It's the fastest way to capture the party apparatus."

Fifth, "distance yourself from Obama. But don't ever look like you hate him. It'll piss off African American voters."

Sixth, "you're good in small groups," he said. "From time to time, show the press some ankle. But not too much."

Seventh, "no one's got the credentials you've got. When you got it, flaunt it." When we were in the White House, we balanced the budget, not like the jerks who came after us and ran up $18 trillion in debt. Make a sharp contrast between this administration and the past and *future* Clinton administrations.

"It's going to draw blood and make some members of the party crazy," he went on. "There's going to be a massive blowback from the Obamas and their troops. But that's too bad. The strategy will work. And that's all that counts. You can't appear to be a continuation of the Obama doldrums. The difference between you and Obama is, he makes promises and doesn't deliver; you promise *and* deliver."

Eighth, have some fun.

Bill stopped.

"What about ninth and tenth?" Hillary asked, half seriously.

"I haven't got to them yet," he said to laughter around the table.

Bill then went down the list of Hillary's probable Republican opponents.

He hoped the Republicans would nominate Scott Walker, the governor of Wisconsin, who took on and beat the public-service unions in his state. Dick Trumka, the president of the AFL-CIO, would love a chance to get back at Walker. Trumka had promised Bill he'd spend hundreds of millions of dollars and put a vast army on the streets to assure a Hillary victory over her Republican opponent.

"I can count on Trumka," Bill said. "People think that because the unions have been losing members they've been losing clout. But that isn't true. Over the past few years, the unions have spent more than $4 billion on political activity. And more than 70 percent of their members vote as their leaders tell them to.

"I've got the strongest relationship with the AFL-CIO that any politician's ever had," he continued. "Obama has huge union support, too, but they don't love him the way they love me. That's the difference. I advise Trumka on strategy. I take his phone calls. I invite him down to Little Rock. I'm always available to the guy. The unions will march with me to hell."

Bill said Jeb Bush, the former governor of Florida, would be a tough opponent.

"Jeb could capture a chunk of the Latino vote," Bill said. "He'd be strong in Nevada, Virginia, Colorado, and Florida. If he had [John] Kasich [the governor of Ohio] on his ticket, he'd be very strong in Ohio and the Rust Belt. That would be a big problem for us. But there's a big downside to Jeb. With Jeb at the top of the Republican ticket, that'll kill all the stupid talk about 'Clinton fatigue.'"

The Republican who worried him the most, Bill said, was Senator Marco Rubio of Florida. "He's young, Hispanic, and a good speaker," Bill said. "He'd pose a generational challenge [to Hillary, who would turn sixty-nine in 2016] and a challenge for the Hispanic vote, which we need to win. But he's still largely unknown to the general public. We've got to destroy him before he gets off the ground."

CHAPTER 21

DINNER WITH LIZ

*[Hillary] has taken money from [Wall Street] groups,
and more to the point, she worries about them as a
constituency.*
—Elizabeth Warren

Bill Clinton had a recurring nightmare.

He told friends that in his mind's eye he could visualize Elizabeth Warren holding forth on a podium in a cavernous convention hall, her eyes on fire behind her rimless glasses, her voice soaring, sounding like she meant every word that came out of her mouth.

Unlike Hillary, who read woodenly from the text of her speeches, Warren was a brilliant speaker. Whether you liked her politics or thought they were loony, you had to admire her oratorical skill. She could pack the galleries and whip an audience into a frenzy.

Warren's opposition to big banks, the top 1 percent of wealthy Americans, and the Keystone XL Pipeline made her the sweetheart of Democratic lefties. No one sang the populist anthem the way she did. She won the Senate seat once held by the late Ted Kennedy—another impassioned orator and darling of the Left—thanks to millions of dollars in donations from outside Massachusetts, mostly from rich environmentalists and Hollywood celebrities like Ben Affleck, Cher, Barbra Streisand, and Jeffrey Katzenberg.

Warren said she wasn't interested in running for president.

Maybe she was and maybe she wasn't. But Bill didn't want Hillary to take any chances. She had been blindsided in 2008 when Ted Kennedy helped Obama steal the nomination from under the Clintons' noses.

Until now, Bill had dismissed the "Draft Warren" movement as a figment of the Fabian wing of the party. But he had loyal Clintonista spies scattered throughout the Democratic apparatus who informed him that Valerie Jarrett was holding secret talks with Warren in an effort to get her to run.

"I've heard from state committeemen about Obama's preference in '16," Bill confided to a close friend. "And they tell me he's looking around for a candidate who's just like him. He wants to clone himself—to find his Mini-Me. And Valerie and Michelle have convinced the president that Elizabeth Warren is his Mini-Me."

Sources close to the Obama White House did not challenge Bill's assessment. They said the president believed Warren would fight like hell to preserve the Obama legacy. He had authorized Jarrett to conduct a full-court press to convince Warren to throw

Israeli prime minister Golda Meir at a Washington, D.C., news conference, December 1971. Bill Clinton planned to repackage Hillary as a strong but loveable older woman— "more Golda than Maggie." (AP Photo)

Hillary waves to crowds during a Fourth of July parade in Gorham, New Hampshire, while her aides herd pesky reporters behind a fat white rope. Her contempt for the press reached paranoid personality disorder symptoms. (Dominick Reuter/Reuters/Landov)

British prime minister Margaret Thatcher at the UN, June 1982. Hillary didn't see the resemblance to either Golda or Maggie and said, "I'm not going to pretend to be somebody I'm not." (AP Photo/Suzanne Vlamis)

Bill and Hillary leave Lenox Hill Hospital in New York City as Chelsea and her husband, Marc Mezvinsky, pose for photographers with their newborn daughter, Charlotte, September 29, 2014. After the birth, Marc's name began appearing on Clinton Global Initiative–related material. (AP Photo/William Regan)

Whitehaven, the $2.85 million mansion that Hillary bought in the fashionable Observatory Circle neighborhood of Washington, D.C., from the $8 million she was paid for her memoir *Living History*. Hillary put her stamp on Whitehaven. It was *her* home. Not Bill's. (*New York Daily News Archive*/Getty Images)

Bill poses during a fund-raiser with a pair of girls from the Moonlite BunnyRanch brothel of Mound House, Nevada, February 2014. Whenever the fancy took him, Bill would take off for another round of pleasures and self-indulgences. (Courtesy of BunnyRanch.com)

Dressed in a blue muumuu, Hillary strolls with Bill and their dog on a beach in the Hamptons, playground of the rich and famous on Long Island, August 2014. Bill liked to sit by the pool and let his legs dangle in the heated water while he schmoozed with friends. (© INFphoto.com/Corbis)

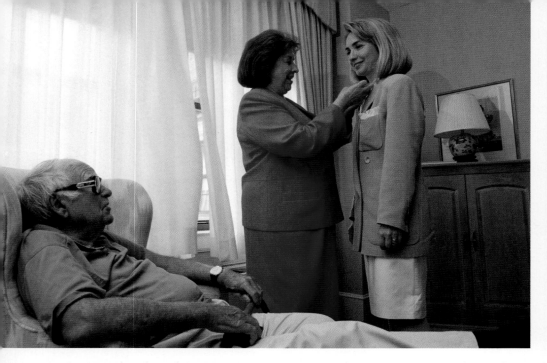

During a break in the 1992 Democratic National Convention, Dorothy Rodham adjusts her daughter Hillary's clothing while Hugh Rodham looks on. Hillary strongly suggested that her father was a sadist who humiliated her mother and beat her brothers. (AP Photo/Ron Frehm)

Bill addresses students in Nairobi, Kenya, May 2015. While on a swing through Africa, he made far-fetched claims about Clinton Foundation fund-raising that ranked right up there with "I did not have sexual relations with that woman … Miss Lewinsky." (John Muchucha/ AFP/Getty Images)

U.S. Senate candidate Hillary Clinton, a lifelong Chicago Cubs fan, tries on a Yankees hat while team owner George Steinbrenner looks on, June 1999. Female participants in focus-group sessions saw through Hillary and described her as "cunning," "pushy," and "cold." (AP Photo/Susan Walsh)

DreamWorks founders (from left) David Geffen, Jeffrey Katzenberg, and Steven Spielberg, October 2004. Most people outside Geffen's inner circle didn't know that he had parted company with Bill and Hillary. "Everybody in politics lies," Geffen told Maureen Dowd, "but [the Clintons] do it with such ease, it's troubling." (AP Photo/John Marshall Mantel)

Democratic presidential candidate Barack Obama gets a big hug from Oprah Winfrey, December 2007. In a dramatic break with precedent, Oprah ditched Hillary and endorsed Obama for president. Her endorsement garnered headlines all over America and was worth more than a million votes. (AP Photo/ Charlie Neibergall)

Hillary's chief of staff Cheryl Mills (left) with Hillary and Senator Patrick Leahy (right) in Haiti, October 2012. While Hillary was secretary of state, her brother Tony Rodham was appointed to the advisory board of VCS Mining, a U.S.-based company that received a gold-mining contract in Haiti. (*Miami Herald*/Getty Images)

Hillary and Obama share the stage at the end of the ABC/Facebook New Hampshire debates, January 2008. Refusing to let Hillary off the hook, Obama threw her some shade and said, "You're likeable enough, Hillary." (AFP Photo/Emmanuel Dunand)

Valerie Jarrett (left), Michelle, and President Obama visit a Miami high school, March 2014. The ruling triumvirs—Obama, Jarrett, and Michelle—worked overtime to undermine Hillary's chances of becoming president. (Reuters/Yuri Gripas)

Jarrett and Hillary have a chat at the Eisenhower Executive Office Building, March 2012. Hillary did not like or trust Jarrett, and she knew that the feeling was mutual. (AFP Photo/Saul Loeb)

Chelsea Clinton and Marc Mezvinsky arrive at a Millennium Network event hosted by Bill Clinton in Hollywood, California, March 2011. Chelsea urged her parents to find a role in the family foundation for her husband. But at first, Bill and Hillary didn't pay him much attention. He wasn't their cup of tea. (Krista Kennell/Sipa via AP Images)

Hillary and Huma Abedin stroll on the Columbia University campus, April 2015. As "Hillary's shadow," Huma kept tabs on Hillary's personal needs—lodging, transportation, meals, and snacks. And she carried Hillary's BlackBerry, which would become a major prop in Hillary's e-mail scandal. (© 247PAPS.TV/ Splash News/Corbis)

Secretary of State Clinton tours the Port of Melbourne in one of her signature pantsuits, November 2010. Bill urged Hillary to get rid of her pantsuits. He never liked that look on her. "Toss them all in the fireplace," he said. But the more Bill complained about her pantsuits, the more Hillary was determined to wear them.
(AFP Photo/Pool/Scott Barbour)

Actress Kate McKinnon plays Hillary in a *Saturday Night Live* sketch, March 2015. *SNL* lampooned Hillary's problem connecting with voters. "What a relatable laugh!" McKinnon said mockingly of Hillary.
(© NBC Universal/ Photofest)

Hillary defends her use of a private e-mail account during a press conference at the UN, March 2015. Her explanation that it was "convenient" not to carry around two phones was laughable. Even the most tech-challenged senior citizen knew you could have two or more e-mail accounts on one phone. (AP Photo/ Richard Drew)

Bill and Hillary slow dance in their bathing suits on the beach in Saint Thomas at the height of the Paula Jones sexual harassment suit against Bill, January 1998. Clinton insiders said that it was unlikely that Hillary's public-relations people would ask her to follow in Michelle Obama's footsteps and break it down in hip-hop style. (AFP Photo/Paul J. Richards)

A terrorist brandishes his rifle as the U.S. compound in Benghazi goes up in flames, September 2011. In a letter to the House Select Committee on Benghazi, Hillary insisted that the only private e-mail address she ever used while secretary of state was hdr22@clintonemail.com. That was a lie. (STR/AFP/Getty Images)

Hillary testifies before the Senate Foreign Relations Committee, January 2013. "Her outburst during the Senate committee hearing on Benghazi—'What difference does it make?'—was in total keeping with her pattern of behavior," said a close Hillary acquaintance. "Something snaps when she's under pressure and emotional stress." (Saul Loeb/AFP/Getty Images)

Lebanese-Nigerian billionaire Gilbert Chagoury and his wife at a Beverly Hills fashion show, 2003. *Investor's Business Daily* reported that Chagoury had a financial interest in keeping Boko Haram off the list of worldwide terrorist organizations. (Star Max via AP Images)

Bill and Canadian mining financier Frank Giustra arrive in Haiti, June 2014. Giustra said he was just one of 1,100 *undisclosed* donors to the Clinton Foundation, most of them foreigners. (AFP Photo/ Hector Retamal)

GreenTech Automotive executive Terry McAuliffe (second from left) jokes with Bill and former Mississippi governor Haley Barbour (right) in Horn Lake, Mississippi, July 2012. McAuliffe sought the help of Hillary's brother, Tony Rodham, in getting special visas for foreigners who promised to invest $550,000 or more in his electric car company. (AP Photo/Rogelio V. Solis)

Bill inspects a new power plant in Caracol, Haiti, October 2012. On the TV screen, he looked haggard and drained of energy. He was sixty-eight years old—by today's standards, still middle-aged—but he looked and acted like an old man. When he wasn't performing for the public—when he let down his guard in private—he looked and acted even worse. (AP Photo/Larry Downing, Pool)

The Clintons' home on Old House Lane in Chappaqua, New York. Several old Clinton hands made the trek to Chappaqua for a crisis meeting when Hillary's campaign was nearly scuttled by a tsunami of scandals. (*New York Daily News* Archive/ Getty Images)

Hillary leaves New York Presbyterian Hospital with Bill and Chelsea following treatment for a blood clot and a concussion, January 2013. She was plagued by blinding headaches. There were incidents on the campaign trail when she felt faint and nearly swooned. Those incidents were kept secret. (Joshua Lott/Reuters/ Landov)

Hillary greets John Kerry prior to his Senate confirmation hearing to replace her as secretary of state, January 2013. Kerry let Hillary know on the QT that Valerie Jarrett was out to sabotage her campaign for the White House. (AP Photo/ Pablo Martinez Monsivais)

Hillary whispers to Senator Elizabeth Warren during a Foreign Relations Committee hearing, January 2013. The Obamas had a powerful ally in Warren, who seemed bent on making mischief for Hillary and the Clinton legacy. (Andrew Harrer/Bloomberg via Getty Images)

Amid a crowd of celebrants, Obama (left) and George W. Bush walk across the Edmund Pettus Bridge to mark the fiftieth anniversary of the Selma to Montgomery civil rights march, March 2015. The reason Bill and Hillary didn't attend the anniversary celebration in Selma was President Obama didn't invite them. (Saul Loeb/ AFP Photo/Getty Images)

Monica Lewinsky arrives at the sixty-ninth annual Tony Awards at Radio City Music Hall, June 2015. When Monica suddenly resurfaced after years of living in obscurity, Jarrett discreetly put out word through intermediaries that the White House would look with favor if the media gave Monica some ink and airtime. (Evan Agostini/Invision/AP)

Convicted pedophile and registered sex offender Jeffrey Epstein hugs his close companion Ghislaine Maxwell. Of all the dodgy characters Bill had consorted with over the years, none was more radioactive than Epstein. (© PatrickMcMullan.com)

Bill yuks it up with David Letterman, May 2015. Asked if he would move back into the White House if Hillary won the election, Bill said "100 percent I'll move back." But according to one of Bill's legal advisers, Bill had no intention of taking up residency in the White House, the way first ladies have traditionally done. (Jeffrey R. Staab/CBS/Landov)

The press chases after Hillary's Scooby Doo campaign van in Iowa, April 2015. Hillary's "unmistakable message [to the media]," wrote *Politico* editor in chief John F. Harris, could be "easily distilled into three short words: Go to hell." (© NBC Universal Archives)

her hat into the ring. With that in mind, Jarrett promised Warren tons of money and organizational support from the White House if she entered the primary campaign against Hillary.

Bill's spies also told him that several members of the Kennedy clan were wooing Warren, too.

Was it possible that the Draft Warren movement could suddenly ignite? If Hillary faltered in Iowa or New Hampshire, would Warren do a Bobby Kennedy and enter the race at the last moment with an army of true believers?

The odds were against it, but you didn't get to be Bill Clinton by leaving things to the whims of chance.

And so, when he and Hillary received an invitation from Robert Kennedy Jr. to visit the Kennedy clan in Hyannis Port, they jumped at the opportunity to do some fence mending.

━━━

The Clintons flew in a private jet to Barnstable Municipal Airport, where they were met by three Secret Service SUVs and a police escort. They were whisked off to the Kennedy Compound, where a catered buffet lunch was waiting for them under a large tent outside the President's House, which Teddy Kennedy Jr. had inherited from his father.

The Kennedy family was split down the middle over whom to back for the Democratic nomination. Robert Kennedy's widow, Ethel, and their eldest son, former U.S. congressman Joe II, favored Elizabeth Warren, while environmental activist Bobby Jr. and his brother Max remained loyal to Hillary.

Despite the death of family patriarch Ted Kennedy, who succumbed to a brain tumor in the summer of 2009, the Kennedys still considered themselves the torchbearers of the Democratic Party. They saw an opportunity to repeat the kingmaker role they played in 2008, when Ted and Caroline Kennedy endorsed Barack Obama.

A sizeable contingent of the Kennedy family turned out for the Clinton lunch: Bobby and his fiancée, actress Cheryl Hines, Ethel, Joe II, Max and his sister Rory, Doug and Bobby Shriver, and Chris Lawford.

"Bill was in full campaign mode," said a source who attended the lunch. "He made a point of talking to every member of the family, shook every hand, and remembered the names of everyone from the youngest to the oldest. Hillary was pretty reluctant about going for a sail on Ted Kennedy's old schooner, the *Maya*, but Bill told her that you couldn't visit the Kennedys and not go for a sail. The outing on the choppy waters of Lewis Bay and Nantucket Sound was pretty rough, and Hillary returned looking a little green around the gills."

—

A week after the Clintons' visit to Hyannis Port, Joe Kennedy invited Elizabeth Warren to the family compound.

"Joe meant Liz's visit to be a counter-move to Hillary's," said a Kennedy family member. "He wanted to expose Liz to the family to gain their support. And sure enough, she came to the compound breathing fire about the need to rein in corporate America.

"Joe thinks Hillary has too many ties with Wall Street," this source added. "He loves Liz because she's a full-throated liberal like his Uncle Ted. She has Ted's voice—loud and angry and triumphant. Joe's talked to some of Liz's advisers and family members, and they are almost unanimous in hoping that she'll give it a try."

But Warren expressed deep reservations.

"Liz said that she's flattered by all the attention and wants to continue the good fight for Teddy's memory," a Kennedy family member said in an interview for this book. "But she says she just doesn't feel up to the grueling battle that a presidential campaign requires. She actually gets breathless when she talks about it.

"Liz is enjoying being in the Senate and has big plans for pushing progressive legislation," this source continued. "It would take a major stumble from Hillary to make Liz change her mind. And even then she's not sure she's up for the battle."

—

When the Clintons received word about Elizabeth Warren's powwow at the Kennedy Compound, they went into damage-control mode. They invited Warren and her husband, Harvard Law School professor Bruce H. Mann, to dinner at Whitehaven.

Hillary and Warren left their husbands in the house while they went for a womano a womano stroll in Rock Creek Park, which bordered the Clintons' property. It was a cool, pleasant evening, and the walk in the woods gave Hillary a chance to weigh Warren's intentions and feel her out to see if she could be bought off.

When the women came back, they washed up and sat down to dinner.

"They served Bill's favorite Italian food, creamed lobster over pasta, from the Filomena Italian Market in Georgetown," said a source who was present at the dinner. "I didn't notice the wines because I wasn't drinking, but they looked like expensive Chiantis to go with the Italian food.

"Bill wasn't feeling well and he took only one bite," this source continued. "He really looked bad—thin, pale, and in pain. He was testy and clearly uncomfortable. During dinner, Warren was guarded about her intentions. She said that doing her job in the Senate was keeping her busy.

"Bill's instinctive feeling, which he later shared with Hillary and a couple of friends, was that in her heart of hearts Warren wanted to run for president, but that, for all her bluster, she didn't have the stomach for it."

PART VI

THE VENDETTA

*Vengeance, oh, vengeance
Is a pleasure reserved to the wise.
To forget a shame or an outrage
Is always base and cowardly.*
—Wolfgang Amadeus Mozart,
"La Vendetta," Act I of Le Nozze di Figaro

CHAPTER 22

WHISPERING CAMPAIGN

After we win this election, it's our turn. Payback time.
—Valerie Jarrett

During the run-up to the 2014 midterm elections, Valerie Jarrett heard that a whispering campaign against Barack Obama was making the rounds of Democratic politicians, donors, consultants, and operatives.

The whisperers were saying that Obama was an albatross around the neck of the party, and that if Democrats running for office knew what was good for them, they wouldn't be seen campaigning with the unpopular president.

The message: Stay away from Obama. He's toxic.

In many parts of the country, especially in the great conservative expanses between the two liberal-leaning coasts, Obama and his policies were generally viewed as harmful. As a result, a lot of Democratic candidates were refusing to accept the president's offer of help.

Jarrett was furious. She refused to trust the findings of the most recent opinion polls, which showed that Obama's popularity was near its all-time low. She said that she detected an element of racism in the polls' results.

"Val told me that the polls were rigged," said a source who was close to Jarrett and spoke to her frequently. "She said the polls counted more Republicans than Democrats, and more whites than blacks. She saw a lot of components—the pundits and the press and racists trying to wrestle control of the party away from Obama. She saw the whole thing as a conspiracy to weaken the president.

"She told Michelle what she had learned, and the two of them took the information to Obama," the source continued. "They told him it was time he grew a pair of balls and got out there and campaigned and talked about hope and the future.

"When Val comes to the Oval with Michelle, Obama knows he's in for it. All of his staff immediately check their smartphones and suddenly remember they're late for an important meeting. The office clears out. Obama sits alone on the couch facing Val and Michelle.

"Michelle usually starts out calm, but her voice can rise when she doesn't seem to be having the effect she wants. The meetings can get very heated. Sometimes they descend into shouting matches. Michelle paces the floor, practically talking to herself.

"It's like they can't wake him up. Val and Michelle don't understand why they can't spark Obama into action and get him to attack the Clintons. They can't even make the man angry. Val said they'd never seen Obama so listless and lacking in fire. He hits a switch, orders a couple of beers, and laughs it off."

Who was behind the whispering campaign?

Was it Bill Clinton, who didn't make any secret of his feelings about Obama?

Obama's failure to act in Syria, a reporter quoted Bill as saying, could end up making him look like a "total fool" and a "wuss."

Or was it Hillary, who was eager to detach herself from Obama's policies on the environment, immigration, and foreign affairs?

In an interview with the *Atlantic*, Hillary criticized Obama's foreign policy in the Middle East, suggesting that it had led to the rise of the Islamic State.

"The failure to help build up a credible fighting force of the people who were originators of the protests against Assad—there were Islamists, there were secularists, there was everything in the middle—the failure to do that left a big vacuum, which the jihadists have now filled," she said.

Asked by the *Atlantic*'s Jeffrey Goldberg what she thought of the slogan President Obama used to describe his foreign policy doctrine—"Don't do stupid shit"—Hillary replied: "Great nations need organizing principles, and 'Don't do stupid stuff' is not an organizing principle."

—

Valerie Jarrett was stunned when she was told of Hillary's remarks. But her immediate reaction was to blame Bill.

"This has Bill Clinton's fingerprints all over it," she said.

She was right. Bill was trying to marginalize Obama and wrest control of the Democratic Party from the sitting president. As a first step, he won over the support of Debbie Wasserman Schultz, the chairman of the party, who transferred her loyalty from the Obamas to the Clintons without so much as a by-your-leave.

As part of Bill's strategy, the Clintons strip-mined the Obama administration of key personnel. Among the Obama advisers who were lured over to Hillary's camp were Joel Benenson, as her chief strategist; Jim Margolis, as her media consultant; Jennifer Palmieri, as her communications director; Buffy Wicks, as a senior coordinator; and Jeremy Bird and Mitch Stewart, as her field directors.

The Clintons replaced Hillary's Sisterhood of the Traveling Pants with what the *Washington Post* called a "frat house" full of former Obama operatives.

These veterans of the Obama political wars were a cold-blooded lot. In pursuit of the nomination and the White House, they were prepared to write off large swaths of independent voters and white working-class Clinton Republicans in favor of a strategy focused on mobilizing the Democratic base. In addition, they were ruthless in their treatment of Hillary's opponents for the nomination. According to a confidential memo that was leaked to me from inside one of the opponent's campaigns, Hillary's frat boys were trying to kneecap the opposition. Here's an excerpt from the memo:

> [Hillary's people] are planning to hold off deciding on the rules and regulations for ballot access in party primaries and caucuses until the last minute when we will have little chance to meet the requirements.... This is the Sopranos rigging the system. And they have enlisted FDR's grandson, James Roosevelt III, as cover in his role as co-chair of the [Democratic National Committee] Rules and Bylaws Committee to steer whatever changes they plan.
>
> And the irony is while accusing the GOP of limiting [voter] access in the general election, they're pursuing just the opposite path for the nomination race, seeking to remove restrictions in the general election while imposing restrictions on primaries and party debates.

The person who leaked that confidential memo was scathing in his description of Hillary's strong-arm methods.

"The Clintons are consciously going out and hiring every person who could possibly work in another campaign," he said. "They're offering them big bucks so that no one else can hire them. They're also shutting off the valve of campaign contributions from potential donors. I've talked to people who want to support another candidate, and they tell me that they're afraid of the Clintons and what the Clintons will do to them if it becomes known that they've given money to someone other than the Clintons. It's a strategy of fear, making people afraid, and it's a strategy that works."

——

The struggle for control of the Democratic Party was at the heart of the blood feud between the Clintons and the Obamas.

When I published *Blood Feud: The Clintons vs. the Obamas* in 2014, some mainstream reporters refused to accept the evidence of such a feud. Others acted as though I had never written *Blood Feud*. For instance, Nicolle Wallace, cohost of *The View*, said that *if reporting were done* on the schism between the Clintons and the Obamas, it could sink Hillary's chances to become president. "[Hillary] and the Obama White House really, really hated each other," Wallace said, as though she were discovering something new. If that came out, she continued, "I think that would confound a lot of Democrats."

However, by the spring of 2015, a cover story in the *New York Times Magazine* titled "The Great Democratic Crack-Up of 2016" linked the words "blood feud" directly to the "Democratic Party" in the opening sentence.

The author of the article, Robert Draper, acknowledged the "identity struggle" and "intraparty disagreements that have been decades in the making…a striking development for a party that has largely kept its internal skirmishes under wraps."

The feud was both ideological and personal.

Ideologically, it pitted so-called "Elizabeth Warren Democrats" against what the *Times Magazine* called "moderates [who] believe the only remedy is for Democrats to refashion themselves as pragmatists who care more about achieving results than ideological purity."

Obama was clearly aligned with the first group, the Warrenites.

Bill and Hillary Clinton, on the other hand, were long associated with moderate elements in the party—people like Robert Rubin, Bill's business-friendly, free-trade former Treasury secretary. Hillary had a reputation as a foreign policy hawk; she once threatened to "obliterate" Iran if it should attack Israel.

The blood feud also reflected the deep and abiding animosity that Barack Obama and Bill Clinton felt for each other. Obama resented the fact that Bill Clinton continued to behave as though *he* should still be president, *not* Obama. Obama bristled when he heard that Bill frequently phoned cabinet secretaries and Democratic leaders in the House and Senate and told them what *he* thought they should do. Obama saw Clinton's efforts to exert influence over the party as more than an encroachment on his prerogatives.

It was personal, not business.

In addition, Obama did not want to see the Clintons return to power, because it would undo plans he had for his post-presidency. After he left office in January 2017, he intended to keep his coalition together and stay active in the real-life political Game of Thrones. A presidential victory by Hillary in 2016 would make that all but impossible.

"Mrs. Clinton's political operation could dominate the Democratic Party for the next decade, controlling the flow of commissions, consulting work and political appointments," noted the *New York Times*.

But was Obama being realistic? After he left the White House, could he continue to have influence over the Democratic Party and push America in the direction of a European-style socialist state?

"It seems highly unlikely," said Henry Sheinkopf, a longtime Democratic strategist, in an interview with the author of this book. "Other than Clinton, there hasn't been a president who's been able to have real influence over his party after he left the White House. Truman couldn't do it. Ike didn't. The Kennedys couldn't. Lyndon Johnson retired as a recluse. Jimmy Carter has had no influence domestically. Perhaps only Ronald Reagan, if he hadn't developed Alzheimer's, might have been able to maintain a position of power."

But Obama had other plans—and so, maybe even more important, did Valerie Jarrett.

▬

Jarrett vowed to seek revenge against the Clintons.

Her first opportunity came when Monica Lewinsky suddenly resurfaced after years of living in obscurity. Jarrett discreetly put out word through intermediaries that the White House would look with favor if the media gave Monica some ink and airtime.

Reporters jumped at the chance.

Jarrett was also the source of leaks to the press about Hillary's use of her private e-mail account and the location of Hillary's e-mail server in Chappaqua. According to someone who spoke directly with Jarrett, the e-mail scandal was timed by Jarrett to hit the headlines just as Hillary was on the verge of formally announcing that she was running for president.

Jarrett was careful to make sure that her fingerprints weren't on the leaks. She used people outside the administration to pass on information to reporters so the story couldn't be traced to her or the White House.

In addition, Jarrett ordered the State Department to launch a series of investigations into Hillary's conduct at Foggy Bottom, including the possible abuse of her expense account, the disbursement of funds, her contact with foreign leaders, and her collusion with the Clinton Foundation.

Altogether, Jarrett launched six separate probes into Hillary's performance at the State Department. She planned to pile on the scandals, one after another, until Hillary sank beneath the wreckage of a ruined reputation.

CHAPTER 23

ON THE QT

[Hillary] will defend, I know, her own record for herself.
It's not my job to do it.
—Secretary of State John Kerry

N one of this took Hillary by surprise.

According to a high-ranking State Department official, Secretary of State John Kerry had let Hillary know on the QT that Valerie Jarrett was out to sabotage her campaign for the White House. Kerry said Jarrett had ordered investigators to do a thorough review of Hillary's State Department papers, and the investigators were also interviewing Foreign Service officers in a hunt for incriminating evidence against Hillary.

There were several reasons that might have explained why Kerry gave Hillary a heads-up.

First, he had mixed feelings about Jarrett. When Kerry was a senator, Slate ranked him as the most vain member of that body, and it wounded his amour propre that Jarrett had not put him forward as Obama's first choice to replace Hillary at State. Instead, Jarrett pushed the nomination of UN ambassador Susan Rice, a close personal friend of both Jarrett and First Lady Michelle Obama. But Rice was sidelined after she appeared on five Sunday talk shows and falsely blamed the deadly attack at the U.S. mission in Benghazi on a "spontaneous" demonstration fomented by an Internet video mocking Islam.

What's more, it was Hillary who introduced Kerry at his confirmation hearing in the Senate. And when Kerry took over at Foggy Bottom, he gave a shout-out to Hillary.

"So here's the big question before the country and the world and the State Department after the last eight years," Kerry said. "Can a man actually run the State Department? As the saying goes, I have big heels to fill."

But all had not been sweetness and light between Kerry and Hillary.

"When Kerry made a comment in 2006 that students should study hard 'and if you don't, you get stuck in Iraq'—something he said when he was considering another presidential bid—Clinton was quick to publicly criticize him," reported the *Boston Globe*. "In 2008, Kerry endorsed Barack Obama over Clinton."

So why was Kerry going out of his way to curry favor with Hillary?

Political insiders suggested that Kerry was trying to stay on good terms with both sides in the Clinton-Obama feud. He needed Obama's support to carry out his job as secretary of state, a cabinet post he had wanted ever since he lost the 2004 race for the presidency. But he was also keeping an eye on the 2016 race—just in case Hillary faltered.

"Kerry is focused on creating a legacy for himself as secretary of state—and he's thinking a lot more about Iran than he is Iowa," the *Boston Globe* noted. "But while he would not challenge Clinton in a primary, he still harbors some presidential ambitions.

"'If she imploded...I gotta believe that this would be something that at least would cross Kerry's mind,' said one Kerry confidant. 'I've never wanted to be president. But my gut tells me it's hard to lose that lustfulness.'"

——

The Clintons had a fifth column of friends in the media who confirmed what Kerry had told Hillary.

"My contacts and friends in newspapers and TV tell me that they've been contacted by the White House and offered all kinds of negative stories about us," one of Bill's friends quoted him as saying. "The Obamas are behind the e-mail story, and they're spreading rumors that I've been with women, that while Hillary was at the State Department she promoted the interests of people and countries who'd done favors for our foundation, and that John Kerry had to clean up diplomatic messes Hillary left behind."

But for all of Bill's anger, he and Hillary were in a quandary about what to do.

If they directed their attacks on Obama, the first black president, they risked alienating the base of the party—blacks, Hispanics, single women, young people—whose support they needed in the coming primaries and general election. On the other hand, how could they allow the investigations of Hillary's tenure at the State Department to go unanswered?

The sticky situation weighed heavily on Hillary.

"She's grinding her teeth at night again," said a friend. "She has a plastic mouth guard so that she doesn't damage and wear out her teeth. And she and Bill are drinking more than usual. When they're out on the campaign trail, they're all right. It's during lulls in the action that the pressure gets to them."

CHAPTER 24

SOMEBODY "O'MALLEABLE"

[Obama is] luckier than a dog with two dicks.
—Bill Clinton, during the 2012 presidential race

After the Democrats took a shellacking in the midterms and the Republicans gained control of both houses of Congress, Bill Clinton gave an interview in which he seemed to pin the blame for the losses on Obama.

Obama's decision to postpone an executive order granting amnesty to millions of illegal immigrants, Bill said, may have been responsible for "a loss of the Hispanic vote."

As far as Obama was concerned, that was the last straw.

He was fed up with being lectured by Bill. He realized that there would be times when he couldn't avoid personal contact with Bill, but he intended to make those occasions as rare as possible.

He ordered a White House aide to call Huma Abedin and schedule a meeting with Hillary. It was made clear that the invitation was for Hillary alone; she was to come to the White House without Bill. He was no longer welcome in the Oval Office.

The meeting with Hillary was set for early December 2014 and was described to the author of this book by several sources—some close to Hillary and others close to Valerie Jarrett. Hillary showed up in black slacks and a tight blue and brown tweed jacket. She was ushered into the Oval Office, where Obama offered her a perfunctory handshake. He motioned for her to take a seat on one of the sofas while he retreated behind the big oak Resolute desk, which has been used by presidents since John F. Kennedy.

Hillary sat there, waiting.

Obama ignored her while he took several phone calls.

Hillary checked messages on her BlackBerry.

After a few minutes, Valerie Jarrett entered the Oval Office unannounced and sat across from Hillary. She made small talk about their families. Hillary responded by lamenting the outcome of the midterms.

Then Michelle came in the same way Jarrett had—unannounced—and took a seat next to Hillary.

Finally, with his reinforcements in place, Obama joined the group. He sat with Jarrett, facing Hillary.

"You must be busy ramping up for your campaign," Obama said to Hillary. "I'm personally glad to not have any more campaigns to run."

Hillary bobbed her head.

"I just want to make it clear that I'm going to be neutral in the primaries," Obama said. "Very neutral until a candidate is chosen."

Hillary tried to say something, but Obama raised a hand to silence her.

"I know Bill's wanted me to throw my support your way, but I don't want to have that argument with him again," Obama said. "I'm just staying out of it. *Period*."

It was obvious to Hillary that he meant *period* literally: it was the end of the discussion.

For the rest of the hour, they touched on the challenge posed by the Islamic State in the Middle East and the trouble Vladimir Putin was stirring up in Ukraine. Then Obama stood up and showed Hillary out of the office.

—

A few days after the meeting, Jarrett met with a friend and filled him in on the "mini-summit" with Hillary.

"After Hillary was gone," the friend said, recalling his conversation with Jarrett, "Michelle and Val congratulated Obama on handling Hillary so well. They were gleeful about Hillary being shut down and walking away with nothing.

"Michelle and Val will go to any lengths to prevent Hillary from becoming president," the friend continued. "They believe that Hillary, like Bill, is not a true-blue liberal. If she gets into the

White House, they believe she'll compromise with the Republicans in Congress and undo Obama's legacy.

"With Obama's approval," this source went on, "Valerie is doing her best to see that somebody who's more simpatico, and whom they can control more than Hillary, gets the nomination. They like Martin O'Malley. Valerie thinks that he would be—in her words—'O'Malleable.'"

Valerie's search for an alternative to Hillary took on added urgency in the summer of 2015 when she received the results of a private poll that she had commissioned of key Democratic Party constituencies, including blacks, Hispanics, youths, and single women. The internal poll showed that Hillary fared poorly among many of the groups that made up the party's base, and that she was therefore a far more vulnerable presidential candidate than most political observers suspected.

If Hillary got the party's nomination, Valerie concluded, there was more than a fifty-fifty chance that she would go down to defeat and lose the White House to the Republican nominee, which would be the worst possible fate for Barack Obama's legacy.

According to a source who discussed the matter with Valerie, she and Obama spent hours going over the pluses and minuses of potential presidential primary challengers to Hillary—both those who had already declared their candidacies (Martin O'Malley, Jim Webb, Lincoln Chafee, and Bernie Sanders) as well as those who hadn't (Joe Biden). Their conclusion: of all the potential candidates, Joe could mount the most potent challenge to Hillary.

The trouble was, Biden had fallen into a deep depression following the death of his forty-six-year-old son, Beau. The vice president was in no condition to launch a primary campaign.

With Obama's approval, Valerie helped Biden seek psychiatric help for his depression. She also began a series of political discussions with Biden at a gingerly pace, trying not to apply too much pressure on him. But she left no doubt that if and when Biden chose to run, he would have the complete support of the Obama White House.

By late summer 2015, as Biden began to emerge from his deep grief and mourning, he gave permission to his chief of staff, Steve Ricchetti, to take the soundings of uncommitted donors and Democratic Party leaders about a possible run.

The soundings came back positive. Ricchetti found that the death of Beau Biden had created a deep pool of sympathy for the vice president.

"What would Beau have wanted Joe to do?" suddenly became a mantra among Biden supporters.

The answer was obvious: Beau would have wanted his father to run.

CHAPTER 25

A SUB ROSA INVESTIGATION

*If an injury has to be done to a man it should be so severe
that his vengeance need not be feared.*
—*Niccolo Machiavelli,* **The Prince**

Several weeks after the Oval Office meeting with Hillary, Valerie Jarrett invited an old friend to spend the night in the Lincoln bedroom. That evening, the friend joined Jarrett, the president, and the first lady in the family dining room.

"We ate on the new White House china service," the friend recalled. "It had deep blue rings that Michelle said were inspired by the waters of Hawaii. She called it Kailua Blue. The family dining room is small by White House standards, and the dinner was pretty informal. No white table cloth. Red and white wine were offered and everybody had a few glasses except Michelle, who drank sparkling water. The president drank a California

Chardonnay. The dinner was a roasted striped bass served with kale and sweet potatoes. Dessert was carrot cake with decaf coffee.

"'We eat healthy here,' the president joked, 'except when Michelle is out of town. Then I order up burgers and fries.'

"The conversation was mostly about the Clintons and the 2016 election. From time to time, the president drifted off the subject and talked about baseball; he didn't think A-Rod should be allowed to catch up with Willie Mays in the official homerun count. But Valerie kept steering the conversation back to the Clinton Foundation's foreign-donor problem and Hillary's private e-mails. I could tell Barack would have preferred to talk baseball. He was also excited about building his presidential library, moving back to Chicago, and enjoying some real downtime.

"'I'm looking forward to spending a hell of a lot of time in Hawaii golfing with friends,' he said.

"Both Michelle and Val thought that the FBI and the Justice Department should be ordered by the president to investigate the Clintons' conflict of interest. Valerie argued that Hillary had deliberately lied to the president about not taking foreign donations for the foundation while she was secretary of state, and that she had ignored warnings about the use of her private e-mail account.

"The president flinched at the idea of an official investigation. He said it would infuriate the DNC [Democratic National Committee] and Hillary loyalists. And it could cost the party the election.

"Val and Michelle got pretty heated.

"'You need to do your duty and order an investigation,' Michelle said. 'Even the goddamn *Washington Post* and the *New York Times* are outraged about the Clintons. [Attorney General Loretta] Lynch isn't going to move on Hillary unless you make it clear that you approve.'

"The president replied, 'The voters don't give a shit about the foundation.'

"Michelle and Valerie looked at each other and rolled their eyes.

"Finally, after a lot of back and forth, they reached a compromise. The president agreed that the Department of Justice would launch a sub rosa investigation going over the known facts of the Clinton Foundation case and the e-mails, and that the attorney general would come back to the president privately within sixty days or so and give her opinion as to whether the situation merited an official investigation.

"It was awkward, but the two women got what they wanted. At least some investigation of the Clinton Foundation would move ahead.

"At that point, the president threw his napkin on the table and went out to smoke an e-cigarette."

CHAPTER 26

MISSING IN ACTION

I'm not invited. I'm not on the A list, haven't been on it in 20 years and my feet have never trod its red fluffy carpets.
—**Nick Mancuso, actor, writer, director, producer, and painter**

Three weeks after Hillary launched her campaign for the White House, President Obama spoke at a celebration marking the fiftieth anniversary of the historic civil rights march from Selma to Montgomery, Alabama. Forty thousand people, including Obama's predecessor in the White House, George W. Bush, gathered in Selma to commemorate "Bloody Sunday," the day in 1965 when police officers with billy clubs beat peaceful protesters, most of them black, as they tried to cross the Edmund Pettus Bridge.

But where was Bill Clinton, "the first black president"?

And where was Hillary, the Democratic Party's likely standard-bearer in 2016?

They were nowhere to be seen in Selma.

"According to people familiar with her thinking, Mrs. Clinton had discussed whether to go [to Selma] several weeks ago, as some of her allies pressed for her to attend," noted the conservative blog *Hot Air.* "People close to the Clintons, who both made note of the Selma event, described them as in a bind regardless of what they did, given that their presence could have made people see the event through a political lens."

But that wasn't the real reason that Hillary and Bill didn't go to Selma.

They didn't go, because they weren't invited.

As part of Valerie Jarrett's vendetta against the Clintons, the White House had left the Clintons off the invitation list.

"Hillary very much wanted to go," said a source who spoke with both Hillary and Bill. "It was a natural photo-op type of event for her. She thought she was denied it because the Obama people didn't want her marching in the front row with two presidents, Obama and George W. It would have made her look like a peer and, by definition, a future member of the President's Club.

"Bill, on the other hand, wouldn't have gone if they had begged him," the source continued. "He said, 'I'm finished dealing with this guy [Obama].'

"Hillary would have even gone alone if she had been asked. She knew she would get shit for not going to Selma. But without a White House invitation it would have been awkward. The Obamas would have done everything but drop banana peels so that she would fall on her ass crossing the Edmund Pettus Bridge."

Instead, Bill, Hillary, and Chelsea went to a Clinton Global Initiative conference at the University of Miami in Coral Gables, Florida. There, Bill officially announced the appointment of Donna Shalala as the new head of the Clinton Foundation. For the privilege of hosting the Global Initiative program, the university shelled out at least $250,000.

While in Florida, Bill and Alonzo Mourning, the former Miami Heat star, and Mourning's wife, Tracy, held a fund-raiser at the Biltmore Hotel in Coral Gables for the Clinton Foundation and the Mourning Family Foundation. Tickets for the event fetched as much as $25,000. Afterward they made appearances at gatherings in South Beach to raise more money. Bill charmed his way through the rooms, posing for selfies.

"As usual, women were all over Bill," said a source who attended the fund-raiser with Bill. "He was flirty with the women, but Tracy and her security people held everyone at arm's length and whisked Bill and Alonzo in and out as quickly as possible."

CHAPTER 27

A TABLOID STAPLE

There were times when I was physically abused to the point that I remember fearfully thinking that I didn't know whether I was going to survive.
—Virginia Roberts, who alleged in court documents that Bill Clinton visited convicted sex offender Jeffrey Epstein's private island, where he witnessed sexual orgies

Her friends claimed that Hillary had mellowed with age. The famous Rodham temper was under control, they said. She didn't vent her spleen or get as physically aggressive as she used to. She didn't poke people in the chest with her forefinger or throw hard objects at their heads.

That was all in the past.

There was a "New Hillary."

These apologists drew a picture of a woman who had the maturity, composure, and self-discipline to be president of the United States. It was a pretty picture, a politically expedient picture, but it bore no resemblance to the Hillary who came barreling into Bill's home office in Chappaqua one evening shortly after the New Year in 2015.

As Hillary later described the scene to friends, she was trembling with rage and could hardly get the words out of her mouth.

"You've thrown us in the crap again!" she screamed. "I've never been this pissed off at you! I don't think you really want me to be president."

Bill looked up over the rim of his eyeglasses, which were perched on the tip of his nose.

"Calm down," he said.

His air of nonchalance only made Hillary angrier, and with a sweeping motion of her arm, she shoved everything off the top of his desk, sending papers and an expensive piece of Chihuly blown glass flying onto the floor.

"*Jesus!*" Bill said.

He got up to retrieve the Chihuly sculpture, which fortunately wasn't damaged.

He put it carefully back on his desk. He had one of the largest private collections of Chihuly glass in the country.

"You don't care about anything but that fucking piece of glass," Hillary said. "This can be as bad as the Lewinsky mess. How can you be so smart and so fucking dumb?"

"What's this all about?" Bill asked.

"It's about Jeffrey Epstein," Hillary said.

—

Of all the dodgy characters Bill Clinton had consorted with over the years, none was more radioactive than Jeffrey Epstein, a convicted pedophile and registered sex offender.

On at least eleven occasions, between 2002 and 2003, Bill flew on a plane owned by the billionaire money manager. According to flight logs for Epstein's customized Boeing 727, Bill was accompanied to Africa by Epstein's close companion, Ghislaine Maxwell, the daughter of the late, disgraced British newspaper tycoon Robert Maxwell. Ghislaine would later be accused of recruiting underage girls for Epstein and tutoring them in the art of erotic massage.

"What [originally] attracted Clinton to Epstein was quite simple: He had a plane (...the Boeing 727, in which he took Clinton to Africa, and, for shorter jaunts, a black Gulfstream, a Cessna 421, and a helicopter to ferry him from his island in St. Thomas)," wrote Landon Thomas Jr. in *New York* magazine. "Clinton had organized a weeklong tour of South Africa, Nigeria, Ghana, Rwanda, and Mozambique to do what Clinton does. So when the president's advance man Doug Band pitched the idea to Epstein, he said sure. As an added bonus, Kevin Spacey, a close friend of Clinton's, and actor Chris Tucker came along for the ride."

A year after the Africa trip, Bill flew to Hong Kong aboard Epstein's plane, which was outfitted with a massage table and was appropriately nicknamed the "Lolita Express." Along for the ride were two young women who were listed on the manifest only as "Janice" and "Jessica." Bill enjoyed the free-and-easy atmosphere on the "Lolita Express" so much that he later used the plane for flights to Moscow, Oslo, Shanghai, and Beijing.

After Epstein was arrested in 2005, Bill reportedly severed ties with the pedophile and with Epstein's alleged procurer, Ghislaine Maxwell.

At least, that was Bill's story.

In fact, the Clinton Foundation accepted a $25,000 donation from Epstein in July 2006. And Ghislaine was a guest at Chelsea Clinton's wedding in 2010.

Bill's relationship with Epstein became a matter of public knowledge when four of Epstein's alleged victims resurfaced in 2011, which was about the same time that Epstein was released from the Palm Beach County Stockade, where he served thirteen months for soliciting a minor for prostitution. By then, Epstein had settled more than thirty cases out of court for undisclosed amounts of money.

Virginia Roberts, one of the alleged victims who had not yet been paid to go away, told the London *Daily Mail* that Epstein had trained her as an underage prostitute and flown her to London for the express purpose of having sex with Britain's Prince Andrew, the second son of Queen Elizabeth. She also charged that Bill Clinton had visited Epstein's one-hundred-acre private island in Saint Thomas, called Little Saint James, where he witnessed sexual orgies, although he himself did not participate.

"I only ever met Bill twice, but Jeffrey had told me that they were good friends," Virginia Roberts, now thirty-one years old, told the British tabloid. "I asked, 'How come?' and he laughed and said, 'He owes me some favors.' Maybe he was just joking, but it constantly surprised me that people with as much to lose as Bill and [Prince] Andrew weren't more careful.

"Bill must have known about Jeffrey's girls," Roberts continued. "There were three desks in the living area of the villa on the island. They were covered with pictures of Jeffrey shaking hands with famous people and photos of naked girls, including one of me that Jeffrey had at all his houses, lying in a hammock."

Bill's attraction to Epstein wasn't entirely over airplanes and sex. He was fascinated by Epstein's connections. The reckless billionaire, who lived in a fifty-one-thousand-square-foot mansion that was reputed to be the largest residential property in New York City, counted among his acquaintances some of the richest and most powerful figures in business and finance—James "Jimmy" Cayne, a former CEO of Bear Sterns; Alan "Ace" Greenberg, the former chairman of Bear Sterns; Marshall Rose, a highly respected real estate developer; and Leslie Wexner, the founder and CEO of The Limited.

Even after Epstein was released from prison in Florida, he was able to allure prominent figures in the worlds of entertainment and television news to his dinner table. One such dinner, organized by the public-relations maven Peggy Siegal in December 2010, included Woody Allen, George Stephanopoulos, and Katie Couric.

I interviewed Epstein by telephone on June 6, 2011, for an article I was writing for *Vanity Fair* about his relationship with Prince Andrew. Epstein pooh-poohed Virginia Roberts's allegations and called them "a 99 percent fabrication." I noted in my article, which appeared in August 2011, that Prince Andrew and Ghislaine Maxwell strenuously denied Roberts's version of events.

Nonetheless, the sordid story brought back memories of Bill Clinton's past tabloid encounters with Juanita Broaddrick, Gennifer Flowers, Paula Jones, Kathleen Willey, Dolly Kyle Browning, Elizabeth Ward Gracen, and Monica Lewinsky.

But this time, Bill wasn't just hurting his own reputation. He was threatening Hillary's chances of winning the White House. The salacious details of the Epstein saga were fresh in people's minds just as Hillary was about to launch her campaign for the presidency. As a headline in the *New York Post* put it: "Bill's Libido Threatens to Derail Hillary—Again."

—

Shortly after Hillary's meltdown over Jeffrey Epstein, Bill set up a video conference call on Skype with Hillary and one of the Clintons' trusted legal advisers.

"Bill was sipping iced tea and pacing the floor in his penthouse apartment in Little Rock," the adviser said in an interview for this book. "He likes to look at you when you talk. As usual, the Clintons weren't in the same place. Hillary was in her study in Whitehaven.

"Bill wanted me to reassure Hillary that the Epstein problem could be contained from a legal point of view," the adviser continued. "Epstein was waffling about paying off some of the girls who were suing him under the Crime Victims' Act. Pressure had to be put on Epstein to settle with the girls so that the problem would go away. Epstein had to be told that bluntly—very bluntly.

"The same was true of the lawyers for the girls. Some of them wanted to make Bill a material witness, depose him, and call him to testify. They had to be contacted and told they couldn't call the former president and put him in a compromising position.

"But I was too close to the Clintons to take on that assignment. Instead, I enlisted a third party, who was removed from Bill and me by several degrees, to make the contacts. It worked. We heard back that Epstein had instructed his legal counsel to bring the problem to a conclusion.

"My assurances didn't seem to placate Hillary. She was furious that the Epstein matter was creating a major distraction from her political plans. 'Can you really make this fucking thing go away?' she asked. 'My head is going to explode if I hear one more thing about this damn degenerate.'

"During the video conference, Bill asked me to fly down to Little Rock. He sent a plane to pick me up, and when I got there I found him on the garden terrace of his penthouse, chipping golf balls into the Arkansas River.

"Bill's assistant, a very pretty blond, maybe twenty, came to fetch him. Two law professors from the University of Arkansas had been summoned to offer their judgment on the Epstein case. They had some well-reasoned opinions, but I could have saved Bill the trouble of bringing them in, since the matter was already being handled.

"But when Bill's in crisis mode, he always feels the need to be surrounded by many people offering many opinions. It's the old college bull session approach. That's the way he ran things when he was in the White House.

"After the meetings with the professors, there were other legal people from the Clinton School of Public Service. All interesting, smart folks.

"Then we went downstairs and Bill purposely walked through the library greeting tourists, shaking hands, posing for selfies, kissing babies. It was something to behold. He is the most natural politician of his time."

PART VII

Shameless, shameless
You know what you have done
You are shameless, shameless
You've got me on the run
Shameless, shameless
You're tearin' me apart
You are shameless, shameless
You're a face without a heart
—Judy Collins, "Shameless"

CHAPTER 28

THE POTEMKIN CAMPAIGN

It makes zero difference how many questions [Hillary]
Clinton has asked average Americans. Like, none. If those
people were running for president, then I would be super-
interested.... But, they aren't. She is.
—**Washington Post** *political reporter Chris Cillizza*

From the outset of her campaign, Hillary adopted a classic
Rose Garden strategy.

That term was first popularized during the election
campaign of 1976, when Gerald Ford spent most of his
time in the Oval Office, which overlooks the Rose Garden, and
limited his travel around the country. In recent years, the term
has come to have a broader meaning: it refers to a candidate who
refuses to hold press conferences and engage in question-and-
answer sessions with reporters.

Hillary's Rose Garden strategy was aimed at making her more
likeable.

"Her aides are planning a different sort of campaign this time around," wrote the *Wall Street Journal*'s Peter Nicholas. "Mrs. Clinton will be meeting with small clusters of voters in diners, coffee shops and private homes. She won't always have a prepared speech in front of her. Her advisers predict voters will see a less scripted, more disarming candidate than was on display eight years ago.... 'She needs to try to humanize herself, because in some ways she's kind of become a cardboard cutout figure,' says Douglas Brinkley, a history professor at Rice University.

"These aren't the first set of Hillary Clinton aides to grapple with the likeability factor," the *Journal*'s Nicholas continued. "For a quarter century, Clinton staffers, at one time or another, have cast about for a formula that would broaden Mrs. Clinton's appeal and combat perceptions that she is an unsympathetic figure."

The failed strategy of the past failed once again.

In the first month of her campaign, Hillary was severely criticized for ducking the media and taking only eight questions from reporters (or thirteen, depending on whom you asked). As Chris Cillizza of the *Washington Post* pointed out, that came to one question every 3.6 days. And most of her answers weren't answers at all.

Some examples:

Q: You lost Iowa in 2008. How do you win this time? What's your strategy?

Hillary: I'm having a great time. Can't look forward any more than I am.

Q: What about campaign finance reform?

Hillary: We do have a plan. We have a plan for my plan.

Q: How do you respond to criticism that your campaign is too staged?

Hillary: This is exactly what I want to do. I want to hear from people in New Hampshire about what's on their minds.

One of the things reporters wanted to ask Hillary was what would happen to the Clinton Foundation if she were elected president.

"Who would be able to raise money for the Clinton Foundation?" Julie Pace of the Associated Press asked. "Could it begin new projects, both at home and overseas? Is there any way it could operate unburdened by conflicts of interest, real or perceived, while one of its founders sits in the Oval Office?"

On these and all other important issues, Hillary remained silent.

Frustrated in its attempt to get access to the candidate, the *New York Times* posted an item on its *First Draft* blog titled "Questions for Hillary Clinton: Immigration." Amy Chozick, the *Times* correspondent assigned to cover Hillary, explained: "This is the first installment of a regular First Draft feature in which The Times will publish questions we would have asked Mrs. Clinton had we had the opportunity."

The *Washington Post* followed suit. It posted an online clock that counted the minutes since Hillary had answered a press question.

In her first thirty days, Hillary did not hold a single campaign event in New Hampshire that was open to the general public. She spent six days on campaign events and seven on fund-raising. She appeared at sixteen fund-raisers in New York, Washington, D.C., and California, raising about $1.1 million from some of the wealthiest people in America—the same 1 percent she excoriated in her speeches.

Before she started running, Hillary had promised she wouldn't campaign like the Empress Catherine the Great of Russia making a royal progress through the provinces.

But that's exactly what she did. Everywhere she went, her handlers erected a kind of modern-day Potemkin village for the TV cameras. She was televised against artful backgrounds chatting with carefully screened schoolchildren and devoted Hillary enthusiasts.

"The reality is that Clinton's avoidance of the press is a product of weakness, not the result of a shrewd campaign bypassing the media because it can," wrote Josh Kraushaar, the political editor for *National Journal*. "She may be avoiding short-term pain by sticking to her script, but she's creating an imperial image of herself that's hard to reverse—and one the media has every incentive to reinforce.

"If the real reason Clinton's handlers don't want her to meet the press is out of fear—fear that she'll sound politically tone-deaf or get caught fibbing—that's as much a sign of her campaign's anxiety as it is a savvy strategy," Kraushaar continued. "The fear of making a mistake extends to her interactions with voters. Most of her appearances so far have been with supporters who have been vetted and prescreened by the campaign."

At one point during Hillary's visit to Council Bluffs, Iowa, her Secret Service chauffeur pulled her Scooby Doo van into a parking spot reserved for the handicapped. The van remained there while Hillary ducked into a meeting with a group of Democratic activists. Before the meeting began, the participants had to hand over their cameras and cell phones.

Hillary left Council Bluffs without a trace.

At a campaign event in Cedar Falls, which was hosted by billionaire Fred Eychaner, who had given more than $25 million to the Clinton Foundation, a reporter finally managed to put Hillary on the spot. Fox News's Ed Henry asked her if she might speak to the press.

Hillary went into her tough-dude mode and mocked Ed Henry for asking the question.

"Yeah," she said with a derisive laugh, "maybe when I finish talking to the people here, how about that? I might. I'll have to ponder it, but I will put it on my list for due consideration."

Her contempt for the press and her consuming fear of exposure reached paranoid personality disorder symptoms during a Fourth of July parade in Gorham, New Hampshire. As she walked down the street, waving to the crowds, her aides kept reporters away from the candidate by herding them behind a fat white rope.

"Spectacle of Clinton as candidate—press being pulled along with a rope," tweeted the *New York Times*' campaign correspondent Maggie Haberman.

"Hang 'em high, Hillary," wrote *Politico*'s Roger Simon. "Hang those pesky reporters who fly around the country to cover your every event in order to quote what you say and what people say to you. Hogtie them! String them up. Or, at the very least, rope-a-dope them."

When Hillary finally agreed to answer questions about her e-mails and the Clinton Foundation, she offered what *New York Post* columnist Michael Goodwin described as "mush." To Goodwin's ear, Hillary sounded like the old Tammany Hall boss George Washington Plunkitt, who defended "honest graft" and said of his riches, "I seen my opportunities and I took 'em."

CHAPTER 29

ON THE "PRECARIOUS LEFT EDGE"

If I don't have this [economic recovery] done in three years, then it's going to be a one-term proposition.
—*Barack Obama, February 2009*

B ill Clinton watched the rollout of Hillary's campaign from his pleasure dome in Little Rock.

Hillary's managers had excluded him from their strategy sessions.

He was out of the loop.

"Hillary has kept Bill on the sidelines of the campaign because she's very adamant about him not being seen as running the campaign," a Clinton confidant said in an interview for this book. "Hillary is very worried about her campaign being seen as a prologue to Bill's third term. She and her campaign managers have agreed on a strategy to keep Bill in the background.

"Naturally, he isn't happy about that," the source continued. "He wants to be in on everything, and it's been driving him crazy to be kept out of the mix. It's a bigger problem than you might imagine. Their marriage is going through one of its periodic rocky periods as a result, and they're going to have to work it out before the general election."

Bill had to follow the campaign on television news broadcasts, just the way everybody else did.

And he didn't much like what he saw.

He cringed at the clumsiness of Hillary's remarks on the stump when she said that saving the U.S. economy would require "toppling" the richest 1 percent of Americans, and that Americans had to change their "religious beliefs" in order to make abortion legal everywhere.

Bill told his advisers that Hillary's Scooby Doo van was "amateurish and silly," and he practically tore out his hair when he heard that the van had been parked in a zone reserved for handicapped people.

When a TV news show ran a grainy surveillance video showing Hillary and Huma Abedin wearing dark sunglasses and stopping for lunch at a Chipotle restaurant in Maumee, Ohio, Bill asked an aide: "What are she and Huma doing? Are they robbing that place?"

But most of all, Bill tried to put a positive light on his status as a virtual nonperson in the campaign. His chief of staff, Tina Flournoy, told reporters that Bill had never intended to hit the campaign trail for Hillary in 2015 or appear with her at fund-raisers.

"If his advice is asked for, he's happy to give it," Flournoy said. But he wasn't asked.

Which left Bill no choice but to do what he always did when he was ignored—make a commotion and grab the spotlight.

While Hillary was doing her "Silent Cal" routine in Iowa and New Hampshire, Bill granted interviews to three TV personalities—Christiane Amanpour on CNN, David Letterman on the *Late Show*, and Cynthia McFadden on NBC News.

In the interviews, he came across as cranky, out of sorts, and not at all the master of shuck and jive. But he wasn't beyond making things up as he went along.

"What does [Hillary] want me to do?" he said, wide-eyed with naiveté. "I have no idea."

In a gross untruth that ranked right up there with "I did not have sexual relations with that woman...Miss Lewinsky," Bill told McFadden about the Clinton Foundation: "There is no doubt in my mind that we have never done anything knowingly inappropriate in terms of taking money to influence any kind of American government policy."

"I'm not in politics," he replied to another McFadden question, apparently forgetting that Charlie Rose had dubbed him "the best political animal that's ever been in American politics."

"All I'm saying," Bill insisted, "is the idea that there's one set of rules for us and another set for everybody else is true."

Bill was so off his game that he didn't recognize that what he said was the opposite of what he intended.

—

But if Bill was ignored by Hillary's campaign, his ideas were not forgotten.

As we've seen, during a get-together with friends on the eve of the campaign, Bill had listed several items that Hillary had to check off if she hoped to win the White House. She had already staked out positions on many of Bill's must-do items, especially "Feed the base red meat."

"Hillary Rodham Clinton," wrote Anne Gearan in the *Washington Post*, "is running as the most liberal Democratic presidential front-runner in decades, with positions on issues from gay marriage to immigration that would, in past elections, have put her at her party's precarious left edge."

Indeed, Hillary was running to the left—and away from Obama's record—as fast as she could.

And with good reason.

Obama had presided over the worst recovery from a recession in modern memory. Despite his promise to "heal" America's political wounds, he bore a great deal of responsibility for making our political system more divisive, not less so. On his watch, the world's respect for America had plunged to its lowest level since World War II.

Judged by almost any yardstick, Obama was presiding over a failed presidency. Even George W. Bush, who left office with poll numbers in the basement, now enjoyed higher ratings than Obama.

And the negative verdict on Obama's performance went double for leaders in Europe, the Middle East, and Asia, who concluded that Obama was the weakest president since Jimmy Carter.

Here were some of the things Hillary said on the campaign trail to distance herself from Obama:

On stop-and-frisk and mandatory sentencing: "Black lives matter.... It's time to end the era of mass incarceration."

On amnesty for illegal immigrants: "If Congress refuses to act [on shielding millions of illegal immigrants from deportation], as president I will do everything possible under the law to go even further [than Obama]."

On same-sex marriage, she tweeted: "Every loving couple & family deserves to be recognized & treated equally under the law across our nation."

On raising the minimum wage, she tweeted: "Every American deserves a fair shot at success. Fast food & childcare workers shouldn't have to march in streets for living wages. "

On abortion: "Deep-seated cultural codes, religious beliefs and structural biases have to be changed."

On free speech by political groups: Hillary said that as president she would apply a litmus test to Supreme Court nominees by making them pledge in advance to overturn the 2010 *Citizens United* decision that allowed corporations and labor unions to spend unlimited funds backing candidates for office.

On income inequality: "The deck is stacked in [wealthy peoples'] favor. My job is to reshuffle the cards."

CHAPTER 30

"A HYDRA-HEADED BEAST"

Bill doesn't talk about a Hillary presidency;
he talks about their presidency.
—Anonymous

Barack Obama was asked at a press conference: "Mr. President...my question to you is do you still have the juice to get the rest of your agenda through this Congress?"

Obama tried to laugh off the insinuation that he was no longer relevant. Quoting Mark Twain, he said the rumor of his demise was exaggerated. But there was no denying the fact that though Obama might be sitting in the Oval Office, Bill and Hillary Clinton had seized control of the political party of which he was the titular head.

Power over the Democratic National Committee (DNC) gave the Clintons unfettered access to the party's money and organization, and, just as important, the final say over the rules and regulations for the upcoming primaries.

As the front-runner for the nomination, Hillary wanted to participate in as few debates as possible so that she could limit her exposure. The head of the DNC, Debbie Wasserman Schultz— a one-time Obama acolyte who had transferred her loyalty to the Clintons—was more than happy to oblige. The DNC indicated that there would be just four primary debates in 2015 (in Iowa, New Hampshire, South Carolina, and Nevada) and only a hand-ful in 2016.

By contrast, there were more than twenty debates during the Democratic primary in 2008—the last time the nomination was up for grabs.

—

As the day of the first debate approached, the level of tension in Whitehaven, Hillary's home in Washington, was palpable. According to people who spoke directly with Hillary, she and Bill considered the upcoming election to be their last hurrah, and they were worried sick that Hillary was going to blow the campaign and destroy the family brand.

The tension gave rise to continual arguments.

"They have always been a family that engages in spirited debates," said a close Clinton source who witnessed many of these arguments firsthand. "Nobody is afraid to be a contrarian or to argue against the conventional family wisdom. That's why they have shouting matches on a regular basis.

"Chelsea has grown up with parents with hot tempers," the source continued. "She's as clever and analytical at arguing both sides of a question as her dad, and she's as volatile as her mom.

"Chelsea gets angry at her father for bullying her mother. Then she gets equally angry with her mom for not taking her dad's advice. It's almost like a family sitcom, except that this family intends to carry on like the characters in the TV series *Shameless* when they get to the White House.

"There's an air of palace intrigue among the three Clintons. They don't completely trust each other. Bill felt blindsided when Hillary brought Donna Shalala in as the CEO of the foundation. He's always been distrustful of the relationship between Hillary and Donna. They have a chemistry that makes Bill suspicious about their motives. He's deceitful by nature, and he assumes everyone else is disloyal, including his wife and daughter.

"Chelsea doesn't like her husband, Marc, cozying up to Bill, which he does all the time. She's jealous of anyone who gets between her and her father. Marc has always felt like the odd man out in the family, and he tries to ingratiate himself with Bill. Hillary is worried that Marc's financial dealings aren't always entirely kosher, and she's ordered a couple of her aides to keep an eye on Marc and report back to her what he's up to.

"Hillary and Bill obviously love their daughter, but they're not comfortable with all of Chelsea's activities. To them, it looks like Chelsea's installing people loyal to her at the foundation, squeezing out Hillary and Bill's people, and that Chelsea intends to establish a coterie of loyalists in Hillary's campaign as well. She's declaring herself as an independent force.

"The relationship among the three of them is extremely complicated. Chelsea's been a good sailor throughout her life, grinning and bearing it while her parents sailed through a sea of scandals and troubles. As a result, she's built up a huge stack of chits with her parents. And she's clever, very clever at leveraging her power with them.

"Hillary's campaign is a hydra-headed beast with different factions vying for control. Bill and Hillary have separate visions of what a new Clinton presidency would look like. Hillary has a long shopping list of incremental good things that can be done for social welfare, immigration, and school reform. Bill has a grand vision of changing the world through big proposals on the international stage.

"Maybe these disparate visions can be made compatible. But I don't think anybody who knows the Clintons sees that as realistic. Hillary may be the boss of bosses, but her husband and daughter are going to control their own teams. The potential for clashes among them is inevitable. I wouldn't want to be Hillary's campaign manager. He's going to have an impossible job."

———

Hillary had other, even more urgent reasons to be tense and anxious.

The scandal surrounding her use of a private e-mail server had escalated out of her control: the matter had been referred to the FBI for investigation, and for the first time in her life, Hillary faced possible criminal charges. According to several close Clinton sources who were interviewed for this book, Hillary was frightened and furious and defiant all at once.

"I noticed that when I talked to her about the e-mail situation, her hands were trembling more than they had in the past," one of these sources said. "It wasn't like Parkinson's by any means, but it was a nervous kind of trembling. Hillary believes that she has to charge ahead and clinch the nomination as quickly as possible before the Justice Department takes any action that might result in criminal charges. The way she sees it, once she clinches the nomination, Obama will have to call off his dogs or he'll be seen as destroying the Democratic Party and ushering in Jeb Bush or Donald Trump. And that would be a disaster.

"That's the Clinton strategy going forward," this source continued. "A full-court press. They are going to spend tons of money early. Drop a nuke on her Democratic opponents and have the Clinton tough guys go bare knuckle. Hillary is convinced the FBI investigation will be very slow and that there is time. Obviously the caucuses and primaries are set in time. But opinion polls are taken every day. She wants to build a brick wall that says she's inevitable. From here on out, the whole Clinton family is in full combat mode."

CHAPTER 31

"IT'S GONE WAY TOO FAR"

*No one is dumb who is curious. The people who don't
ask questions remain clueless throughout their lives.*
—Neil deGrasse Tyson

Barack Obama could hardly contain his excitement.

"When I get to Ethiopia," he said one summer evening during dinner in the family quarters of the White House, "I'm actually going to touch the bones of Lucy."

He was referring to his upcoming trip to Africa and the 3.2-million-year-old fossilized bones of *Australopithecus afarensis*, the most complete skeleton of an early human ancestor ever discovered.

Lucy was often called "the grandmother of humanity," and Obama was thrilled that she had been found in Africa, which he considered to be his ancestral home, and that he would be the first American president to handle Lucy's bones.

However, his dinner companions—Michelle Obama and Valerie Jarrett—did not share his excitement. Neither of them planned to accompany the president on the Africa trip, and in any case they were more interested in talking about a far more pressing issue than Lucy's bones.

They were preoccupied with Hillary Clinton, her mounting scandals, and her race for the presidential nomination.

According to sources who spoke directly with Jarrett about the dinner conversation, she raised the dreaded possibility that Obama might be forced to support Hillary if none of the other Democratic candidates could rough her up in Iowa and New Hampshire and knock her out of the primary race.

Obama shook his head and said, "I can't get behind that woman and I refuse to spend time with Bill."

—

Valerie Jarrett gave Barack and Michelle Obama an update on Hillary practically every night of the week.

The Obamas were obsessed with Hillary's cascading e-mail scandal. They pressed Jarrett for information. They wanted to know everything—Hillary's poll numbers, how she was coping, what Bill was up to, how Hillary intended to escape from the e-mail trap of her own making.

While Jarrett gave her briefing, the president paced, his head bowed, deep in thought. Jarrett was happy to see Hillary in trouble. Obama wasn't so sure. He felt a great deal of animosity toward both Clintons, and he smiled when Jarrett told him of Hillary's latest travails, but he didn't want to see the Democratic Party lose the White House.

"It's all her own fault," he repeated over and over, according to sources who spoke to Jarrett. "Bill should have advised her better. He should have made her goddamn behave, follow the rules."

"There's nothing we can do now about any of this," Jarrett said. "It's going to be in the hands of the Justice Department. You can't be seen to interfere. It's gone way too far."

Barack plopped down in a chair and let out a sigh.

"Dumb, dumb, dumb," he said. "Just goddamn dumb."

Jarrett disagreed.

"It's not dumb," she said. "It's arrogance. The Clintons think the rules don't apply to them. Bill's even said so in exactly those words."

Jarrett then raised the possibility that Obama could give Hillary a presidential pardon at the end of his term if she was facing criminal charges.

But Obama was noncommittal on the subject of a presidential pardon.

Jarrett said she was operating on the assumption that Hillary was going to falter during the nominating process and that the White House needed to have an alternative in place before it was too late.

"I'm trying to light a fire under Joe [Biden]," she said. "Joe's loyal. He'll listen to you and take your advice. Unlike Hillary, he's faithful and dependable. He knows he owes you big time. A win by Joe would be confirmation that you've had a successful presidency."

Obama looked at Michelle.

They were both smiling.

"Get to work on Joe," Obama told Jarrett.

THAT OLD CAR SMELL

*[John F.] Kennedy was, whether for good or bad, an
enormously large figure. Historically, he was a gatekeeper.
He unlatched the gate and through the door marched
Catholics, blacks, and Jews, and ethnics, women, youth,
academics, newspersons, and an entirely new breed of
politician who did not think of themselves as politicians—
all demanding their share of the action and the power in
what is now called participatory democracy.*
—*Theodore H. White*, **The Making of the President, 1960**

Forty-eight years after JFK's assassination, which many historians mark as the moment America lurched to the left, a new cultural revolution is convulsing our country.

Today, America is witnessing upheavals in communications, technology, globalization, demographics, popular entertainment, financial markets, industry, and commerce. And all of this is having a profound impact on how we order our lives—what we consider morally right and wrong, acceptable and unacceptable, normal and abnormal.

A "new normal" is sweeping across America, turning long-accepted standards and codes of behavior upside down.

- Support for same-sex marriage has doubled over the past decade to 60 percent.
- A majority of Americans support the legalization of marijuana.
- In many communities, the police, not the criminals, are considered the problem.
- The percentage of adults who describe themselves as Christians has dropped by nearly 8 percentage points in the past seven years.
- Nearly a quarter of all Americans describe themselves as atheists, agnostic, or "nothing in particular."
- In less than thirty years non-Hispanic whites will no longer make up a majority of Americans.
- More than half the births to women under thirty occur outside marriage.

"Has American culture become gross, coarse, vulgar?" writes author Stan Latreille, expressing the feelings of perhaps a majority of Americans, or at least a majority of those over the age of forty. "If I say yes, I no doubt will be dismissed as an old fogey. Well, I do say yes, so there. And if you disagree, I say you are blind, deaf, zoned out or just plain stupid."

Examples of the coarsening of America abound.

- Kim Kardashian is celebrated for balancing a champagne glass on her rear end.

- Bruce Jenner, once the picture of masculinity, is canonized for being castrated.
- Summer's Eve feminine-care company runs a video on its website and YouTube showing a talking vagina.

And Americans themselves seem coarser, grosser than previous generations.

- The average American woman now weighs the same as the average American man did in the 1960s.
- Tattoos—once limited to sailors and members of biker gangs—now disfigure more than a third of all Americans under the age of thirty.
- Nearly a third of those under thirty have a body piercing someplace other than the lobe of their ears.
- Within living memory, men wore ties to baseball games; today many people dress, even at work, as if in imitation of Shaggy from *Scooby-Doo*.
- According to a study from professors at Georgetown University's McDonough School of Business and the Thunderbird School of Global Management, employees are now twice as likely to experience rude behavior at an office as they were in 1998.

Conservatives have every reason to be alarmed by the decline in American appearance and behavior, manners and morals. Along with the Roman orator Cicero, we say, "*O tempora, o mores,*" which translates to "Alas the times, and the manners."

"I am glad that I'm not raising kids today," Supreme Court Justice Antonin Scalia told *New York* magazine. "One of the things that upsets me about modern society is the coarseness of manners. You can't go to a movie—or watch a television show for that matter—without hearing the constant use of the F-word—including, you know, *ladies* using it."

Fifteen years ago, Jacques Barzun, the brilliant conservative cultural critic and historian, wrote a book titled *From Dawn to Decadence* in which he lamented the direction in which our culture was headed.

> The cruel, perverse and obscene [is] more and more taken for granted as natural and normal.... The attack on authority, the ridicule on anything established, the distortions of language and objects, the indifference to clear meaning, the violence to the human form, the return to the primitive elements of sensation, the growing lists of genres called "Antis"...have made Modernism at once the mirror of disintegration and an incitement to extending it.

Things have gone downhill since then. Conservatives rightly fear that decadence will lead to the fall of the United States just as surely as it led to the fall of Rome.

Meanwhile, the chasm between conservatives and liberals grows wider by the day. We live in a house divided. This profound difference between people on the Right and Left will have to be managed with diligence if our country is not to fragment and fall apart. Great leadership will be required. This, not income inequality, is the moral issue of our time.

Thus, it is altogether fitting and proper to ask: Is Hillary Clinton the woman for these times?

Can she, as George H. W. Bush once promised to do, make this a "kinder, gentler nation"?

Can she, as George W. Bush described himself as governor of Texas, be "a uniter, not a divider"?

Can she reverse America's decline?

Is she fit to lead?

Barack Obama for one certainly doesn't think so.

He believes that voters will be looking for a "fresh start" when they go to the polls in 2016.

"I think the American people, you know, they're going to want—you know, that new car smell," he told *This Week*'s George Stephanopoulos.

It didn't take a high-paid political consultant to parse the president's meaning. To him, Hillary Clinton represents that *old* car smell.

■

Many of the people I interviewed for this book found themselves agreeing with Obama on the subject of Hillary's staleness.

It would be easy to dismiss this point of view if only conservatives expressed it. But liberals I spoke with seemed almost as

nervous as conservatives about the prospect of placing the hon-
orific "Madame President" in front of Hillary's name. Even
among those who said they planned to vote for her, many
acknowledged that she was a badly flawed candidate whose lack
of accomplishments, serial scandals, absence of shame, unlikeability, and clumsiness as a campaigner could doom her designs
on the presidency.

"Nobody wants to go to a fund-raiser and get another picture
with her," a jaded Hollywood supporter of Hillary told the *New
York Times*' Maureen Dowd. "But we have to figure out how to
get her [to the White House]."

"The joke circulates in Hollywood," Dowd continued, "that
Hillary is like Coca-Cola's Dasani water: She's got a great distribution system, but nobody likes the taste."

"It's a long record going back over decades of questionable
ethical practices," said former Rhode Island governor and U.S.
senator Lincoln Chafee, the longest of long shots in the Democratic primary scrum. "People groan when I bring up Whitewater and all these things, the Rose Law Firm records; it seems like
it never stops. Now, we are into the tenure of secretary of state
and the emails and of course the Clinton Foundation donations
at the same time the State Department is making critical decisions, combined with some of those donations by the Clinton
Foundation. It's just too close and too many ethical questions."

Hard numbers backed up Chafee's concern about Hillary's
integrity. As soon as she announced her campaign for president,
an NBC/*Wall Street Journal* poll reported that her "unfavorables"
jumped six points. She fared even worse among younger

Democratic voters. Her "favorability" with that cohort had dropped by 15 percent since 2007.

Virtually all of the Democrats I talked to said that Hillary would benefit from some healthy competition in the primaries. They yearned for Elizabeth Warren, either because she, unlike Hillary, was, in their estimation, "the real thing," or because she would make the Democratic primaries a true contest. These Democrats were despondent when Warren withdrew from the race, leaving Bernie Sanders, the former socialist mayor of the People's Republic of Burlington and current U.S. senator from Vermont; Martin O'Malley, the tax-and-spend former governor of Maryland; and the aforementioned former liberal Republican Lincoln Chafee as the last men standing. None of them appeared to be up to the challenge of toppling Hillary.

It wasn't only rank-and-file Democrats who harbored uneasy feelings about Hillary. As readers will remember, influential figures in the Democratic Party—elected officials, party bosses, and big donors—were also voicing reservations about Hillary, although they did so sotto voce so Hillary wouldn't hear. This anti-Hillary sentiment was especially alive and well in the White House, where the ruling triumvirs—Barack Obama, Valerie Jarrett, and Michelle Obama—were working overtime to undermine Hillary's chances.

The Obamas had a powerful ally in Elizabeth Warren, who seemed bent on making mischief for Hillary and the Clinton legacy.

"Warren has suggested that President Bill Clinton's administration served the same 'trickle down' economics as its Republican predecessors," wrote David Frum, a former speechwriter for George W. Bush and now a senior editor at the *Atlantic*.

"Warren has denounced the Clinton administration's senior economic appointees as servitors of the big banks.

"Warren has blasted Bill Clinton's 1996 claim that the era of big government is over and his repeal of Glass-Steagall and other financial regulations.

"Warren has characterized Hillary Clinton herself as a conscienceless politician who betrayed her professed principles for campaign donations."

Warren's strategy was clear: she wanted to force Hillary to renounce her "centrist" past and move further and further to the left.

And the strategy was working.

"[Hillary] is so terrified of losing Iowa, and she is so terrified that even if she wins the Iowa caucuses that some liberal does well enough to wound her that it will hurt her chances, that's forgetting the fact that there's a general election to come if she's the nominee," said Bloomberg Politics editor Mark Halperin. "She's terrified of the left and it's showing on a range of issues. Wall Street won't hold her accountable to it but she, I think, is creating a lot of trouble for herself and it's only just begun."

Hillary was beginning to sound like Warren's ventriloquist dummy.

Did Warren declare, "The game is rigged"?

Hillary said, "The deck is stacked" in favor of the rich.

Did Warren say drastic measures had to be taken to tackle income inequality?

Hillary said that saving the American economy from disaster would require "toppling" the 1 percent.

Did Warren favor paid family medical leave?

So did Hillary.

Did Warren call for a constitutional amendment to outlaw "big money" in politics?

So did Hillary.

Did Warren want to double the minimum wage to fifteen dollars an hour?

Mega-dittos from Hillary.

"On the party's favorite issue of income inequality, Clinton is the poster child for what Democrats believe is wrong with the United States," wrote Ed Rogers, a contributor to the *Washington Post*'s *PostPartisan* blog. "If she is the Democratic nominee in 2016, how will the party standard bearer rationalize her gargantuan haul of cash over the past few years? How can she reconcile her past with her platform?

"There are a lot of questions that Clinton will have to answer....

"Even the famous Clinton gall and lack of shame will make explaining some of this with a straight face impossible."

———

In the course of researching this book, I spoke with many people who were ardent Hillary defenders. As far as I could tell, their arguments in her favor boiled down to three main points.

- As one supporter put it, Hillary's "magnitude of experience...dwarfs any of her potential opponents in 2016."
- The time is long overdue for a woman to be president.
- Buy one (Hillary) and get one free (Bill).

Each of these arguments was seriously flawed.

- Hillary's sum total of "experience" can be tweeted in 140 characters or less: HillaryCare, Monica cover-up, Iraq war vote, bungled 2008 campaign, Russian reset, Benghazi, deleted e-mails, selling favors at State.
- "Becoming the first female president is a worthy goal," writes a *Washington Post* columnist. Perhaps. But becoming a *great* president is a far worthier goal. The essential point is this: Americans should not hire a president on the basis of affirmative action.
- Buy Hillary and get a free Willy? We tried that once before. It ended with a president whose license to practice law was suspended by the Arkansas Bar, and who was impeached by the House of Representatives—only the second president in history to suffer that ignominy. Do we really want the Clinton circus back to town?

And so, the fundamental question Americans will face when they go to the polls to pick their next president is this: Have our standards and morals declined to the point that we will elect someone who is so shameless that she lies without a tinge of guilt, and so untrustworthy that she engages in massive cover-ups?

How we answer that question on November 8, 2016, will determine our nation's future.

What difference does it make?

Plenty.

AUTHOR'S NOTE

*I always cheer up immensely if an attack is particularly
wounding because I think, well, if they attack one
personally, it means they have not a single political
argument left.*
—*Margaret Thatcher*

Like all my previous books dealing with Hillary Clinton—
The Truth about Hillary (2005), *The Amateur: Barack
Obama in the White House* (2012), and *Blood Feud: The
Clintons vs. the Obamas* (2014)—this is a reporter's book.

It is based largely on interviews with people who were present
at events they describe or with friends and confidants to whom
they spoke while memories were still fresh.

Many of these people spoke to me on the condition of anonymity. They did so either because they were not authorized to
speak on the record or, more commonly, because they feared that
if their identities became known, they would become the target
of revenge and retaliation.

All contemporary political books use information from anonymous sources to tell important stories that otherwise would go unreported. Bob Woodward, an icon of American journalism, uses unnamed sources both in his reporting for the *Washington Post* and in his books. So do John Heilemann and Mark Halperin, who have used *only* anonymous sources in their *Game Change* books.

In gauging the trustworthiness of an anonymous source, readers are asked to rely on the character and reputation of the reporter who quotes or paraphrases the source. Everything depends on the reporter's experience, judgment, and track record.

After nearly six decades as a journalist, including seven years as foreign editor of *Newsweek*, ten years as the editor in chief of the *New York Times Magazine* (during which time the magazine won its first Pulitzer Prize), and twenty-six years as a contributing editor for *Vanity Fair*, I take this burden of trust seriously.

Whenever possible, I have tried to use more than one source to reconstruct a scene or dialogue. Several of my sources were interviewed multiple times (in one case, twenty-four times) to check for accuracy and consistency.

I'm often asked by readers, "How come your books contain so much provocative material that no other authors have? How do you get your stuff?"

There are several answers to that question.

For one thing, over the past decade my talented researchers and I have cultivated unique sources inside the Clinton and Obama camps. Unlike authors who base their information on interviews with "official" sources—press secretaries, campaign advisers, paid political operatives, elected representatives, government appointees, bureaucrats, retired officials—my sources can more properly be classified as "private."

These longtime personal friends and associates hang out with the Clintons and Obamas and are privy to information that is unavailable to official sources. These private sources are invited to intimate gatherings; they share meals and family time together with the Clintons and Obamas; and they speak frequently to the Clintons and Obamas on the phone. They are part of discussions that take place beyond the ken of official sources.

For their own sometimes-complicated reasons, these private sources want to speak with my researchers and me in order to make certain things known. They share the common human desire to brag about their connections to the high and mighty. It makes them feel important and powerful. They have what amounts almost to a compulsion to tell someone that they are in the know. Over many years they have become comfortable talking anonymously to me, knowing that I will never betray their trust and make their identities known.

Virtually all of these private sources have an agenda. Among the Clintons' friends, there are those who are closer to Bill than to Hillary, or vice versa. Among the Obamas' friends, some favor Michelle over Barack. These people try to shape the narrative of my books in ways that benefit their favorites—sometimes even at the expense of their favorite's spouse.

Finally, many people jump at the chance to settle scores. Speaking to an author anonymously gives them the opportunity to aggrandize themselves at the expense of others without jeopardizing their standing in the corridors of power. They often try to make a point *against* someone as well as *for* someone by describing conflicts and confrontations that take place behind the scenes.

It's my job as a reporter to weigh the accuracy of the testimony I'm given, test it where possible, and then present it to you, the reader, for your judgment.

—Edward Klein
New York City
August 2015

NOTES

PROLOGUE: "CALL OFF YOUR DOGS"

she was being persecuted: Interviews with people who spoke directly
with Hillary about her meeting with the president. All sources
requested anonymity.

"He has a visceral dislike of me": Ibid.

Obama dreaded the prospect: Interviews with people who spoke
directly with Valerie Jarrett and who requested anonymity.

"One way or another": Ibid.

"At first, Hillary pretended not to care": Ibid.

"He was almost being deliberately dense": Interview with an
anonymous source who spoke about the Oval Office meeting with
Hillary.

"What I want for you to do is call off your fucking dogs": Interviews with several anonymous sources who spoke directly to Hillary and Jarrett about the meeting.

"There is nothing I can do": Ibid.

PART I: A HELL OF A MESS

CHAPTER 1: "MORE GOLDA THAN MAGGIE"

One evening while they were having drinks with friends: Interview with a friend of the Clintons who requested anonymity.

Spielberg let her use his corporate apartment: Branden Keil, "Is Spielberg Pad Now 'Hillary Hilton'?," *New York Post*, October 1, 2000, http://nypost.com/2000/10/01/is-spielberg-pad-now-hillary-hilton/.

CHAPTER 2: #GRANDMOTHERSKNOWBEST

"dream house": John Heilemann and Mark Halperin, *Game Change: Obama and the Clintons, McCain and Palin, and the Race of a Lifetime* (New York: Harper Perennial, 2010).

"fortress of solitude": Amie Parnes, "Where Does Hillary 2016 Begin? In This Washington Home," *Hill*, February 20, 2015, http://thehill.com/homenews/campaign/233274-hillarys-whitehaven-home-is-heart-of-nascent-campaign.

The Barbara Lee Family Foundation: Barbara Lee Family Foundation/ Lake Research Partners, "Pitch Perfect: Winning Strategies for Women Candidates," November 8, 2012, http://www.barbaralee foundation.org/wp-content/uploads/BLFF-Lake-Pitch-Perfect-Wining-Strategies-for-Women-Candidates-11.08.12.pdf.

"Speech practice": Interview with a close Hillary friend who requested anonymity.

Like the Underwoods: Ibid.

CHAPTER 3: THE KING OF LITTLE ROCK

Sometimes, Hillary told friends: Interviews with several of Hillary's friends, who requested anonymity.

"The worst case scenario for the foundation": Kenneth P. Vogel, "Clinton Foundation in Campaign Tailspin," *Politico*, April 30, 2015, http://www.politico.com/story/2015/04/clinton-foundation-bill-hillary-chelsea-117505.html.

"a media whack-fest": Ibid.

"I gotta pay our bills": Daniel Henninger, "I Gotta Pay Our Bills," *Wall Street Journal*, May 6, 2015, http://www.wsj.com/articles/i-gotta-pay-our-bills-1430953025.

The Clintons failed to report: Josh Gerstein, "Hillary's Speech Disclosures Come under Fire," *Politico*, May 20, 2015, http://www.politico.com/story/2015/05/hillarys-speech-disclosures-come-under-fire-118147.html.

The other nine dollars: Kyle Smith, "Would a Clinton Lie to You?," *New York Post*, May 3, 2015.

"This data": Jonathan S. Tobin, "Is the Clinton Foundation Really a Charity?," *Commentary*, April 30, 2015, https://www.commentarymagazine.com/2015/04/30/is-the-clinton-foundation-really-a-charity/.

"Bill told me that if Hillary is elected president": Interview with one of Bill Clinton's closest advisers who requested anonymity.

"There is a social function to the first lady's role": Francesca Chambers, "Chelsea Clinton Could Take on Role of First Lady If Hillary Wins, White House Expert Says," *Daily Mail* (UK), May 12, 2015, http://www.dailymail.co.uk/news/article-3078415/Chelsea-Clinton-role-lady-Hillary-wins-White-House-expert-says.html.

CHAPTER 4: INTIMATIONS OF MORTALITY

Instead of getting a bounce from her road trip: Michael Barone, "Clinton Defenders Advance an Unpersuasive Argument," *Washington Examiner*, April 30, 2015, http://www.washington examiner.com/clinton-defenders-advance-an-unpersuasive-argument/article/2563730.

"Everybody thinks I'm about to die": Interview with a close Clinton source who requested anonymity.

"The recent stuff in the papers": Ibid.

According to Doctor Bardack: Brianna Keilar and Dan Merica, "Clean Bill of Health: Hillary Clinton's Doctor Says 2012 Health Scare Resolved," CNN Politics, July 31, 2015, http://www.cnn.com/2015/07/31/politics/hillary-clinton-health-tax-release/.

"She is exhausted and depressed": Ibid.

Bill was so concerned: Interview with a cardiologist who requested anonymity.

"Most politicians are reluctant": Ibid.

Hillary admitted to one of her best friends: Interview with a close Clinton friend who requested anonymity.

"But she told me that there was no need": Ibid.

"Bill told me that he tiptoed": Interview with a close friend of Bill Clinton who requested anonymity.

"Donna was one of Hillary's closest friends": Interview with a close Clinton friend who requested anonymity.

"His attention seemed to wander": Ibid.

PART II: THE GREAT PRETENDER

CHAPTER 5: THE MISANTHROPE

"without her husband's connections": Camille Paglia, "Hillary Clinton's Candidacy Has Done Feminism No Favours," *Telegraph* (UK), May 24, 2008, http://www.telegraph.co.uk/comment/personal-view/3558713/Hillary-Clintons-candidacy-has-done-feminism-no-favours.html.

She also profited from the *votes Bill bought*: Michael Goodwin, "The Kevlar Clintons," *New York Post*, May 31, 2015.

She was appointed secretary of state: Betsy McCaughey, "Hill's Coattail Career," *New York Post*, March 23, 2015.

"Some visitors to the Rodham home": Edward Klein, *The Truth about Hillary* (New York: Sentinel, 2005).

"Among both relatives and friends": Roger Morris, *Partners in Power* (Washington, DC: Regnery Publishing, 1996).

Hillary suggested that her father was a sadist: Hillary Rodham Clinton, *Living History*, reprint ed. (New York: Scribner, 2004).

In all cases of narcissism: Henry Sussman, *Psyche and Text*, SUNY Series in Psychoanalysis and Culture (State University of New York Press, 1993).

"Can you be a misanthrope": Jeff Gerth and Don Van Natta, *Her Way: The Hopes and Ambitions of Hillary Rodham Clinton* (New York: Little, Brown, 2007).

"When the stress": Ibid.

"the archetypal…progressive intellectual": Andrew Roberts, "Among the Hagiographers," *Wall Street Journal*, updated March 26, 2011, http://www.wsj.com/articles/SB1000142405274870352900 4576160371482469358.

"You can argue": Interview with Doctor Robert Cancro, January 29, 2015.

"In her personal life": George Packer, "The Choice," *New Yorker*, January 28, 2008, http://www.newyorker.com/magazine /2012/10/29/the-choice-8.

"subterfuge and eliding": Carl Bernstein, *A Woman in Charge: The Life of Hillary Rodham Clinton* (New York: Vintage, 2008).

"When she's alone": Interview with an anonymous source.

"She freely admits": Interview with an anonymous source.

CHAPTER 6: "I'VE ALWAYS BEEN A YANKEES FAN"

During Bill Clinton's 1992 presidential campaign: Alana Goodman, "The Hillary Clinton Papers: Archive of 'Closest Friend' Paints Portrait of Ruthless First Lady," Washington Free Beacon, February 10, 2014, http://freebeacon.com/politics/the-hillary-papers/.

"I know that no matter what I did": Michael Kelly, "Saint Hillary," *New York Times Magazine*, May 23, 1993, http://www.nytimes.com/1993/05/23/magazine/saint-hillary.html.

Two years later: Dan Friedman, "Secret Pointers Hillary Clinton Received as First Lady Revealed in Newly Released Documents," *New York Daily News*, February 28, 2014, http://www.nydailynews.com/news/politics/hillary-clinton-advice-likeable-secret-memos-article-1.1706886.

"The outreach would be enormous": Peter Nicholas, "Clinton Campaign's Challenge: Make Her 'Likable,'" *Washington Wire* (blog), *Wall Street Journal*, April 12, 2015, http://blogs.wsj.com/washwire/2015/04/12/clinton-campaigns-challenge-make-her-likeable/.

"I'm a proud woman": William J. Clinton Library Archives.

In 1999, Hillary's staff sent her: Ibid.

"She's duplicitous": Edward Klein, *The Truth about Hillary* (New York: Sentinel, 2005).

Female participants in the campaign's: Elizabeth Kolbert, "The Student," *New Yorker*, October 13, 2003, http://www.newyorker.com/magazine/2003/10/13/the-student.

By her third year in the Senate: Jennifer Senior, "President and Mr. Clinton," *New York* magazine, February 21, 2005.

"Hillary told [Obama]": Robert Gates, *Duty: Memoirs of a Secretary at War*, reprint ed. (New York: Vintage, 2015).

CHAPTER 7: A NEAR-DEATH EXPERIENCE

"Queen of All Media": "Is Oprah the Queen of All Media?," National Public Radio, transcript, May 24, 2011.

A study by two Maryland economists: Brian Stelter, "Oprah Worth a Million Votes to Obama?," *New York Times*, August 11, 2008, http://www.nytimes.com/2008/08/11/business/worldbusiness/11iht-11oprah.15161325.html.

On May 7, 1999, two of President Clinton's: ARMS E-mail System, William J. Clinton Presidential Library, memo dated May 7, 1999.

"People in the Clinton administration": Interview with a close Oprah associate who requested anonymity.

On display in the 13,600-square-foot mansion: *Private Wealth*, June 6, 2012.

"It's not a very big thing to say": Maureen Dowd, "Obama's Big Screen Test," *New York Times*, February 21, 2007, http://www.nytimes.com/2007/02/21/opinion/21dowd.html.

"Americans of all political persuasions": William Safire, "Blizzard of Lies," *New York Times*, January 8, 1996, http://www.nytimes.com/1996/01/08/opinion/essay-blizzard-of-lies.html.

"Mrs. Clinton has embarked this week": Patrick Healy, "After Delay, Clinton Embarks on a Likability Tour," *New York Times*, December 19, 2007, http://www.nytimes.com/2007/12/19/us/politics/19clintons.html.

"Maybe they just don't like me": John Heilemann and Mark Halperin, *Game Change: Obama and the Clintons, McCain and Palin, and the Race of a Lifetime* (New York: Harper Perennial, 2010).

"The feminist debate that raged two decades ago": Timothy Noah, "The Politics of Weeping," Slate, January 7, 2008, http://www.slate.com/articles/news_and_politics/chatterbox/2008/01/the_politics_of_weeping.html.

"I get really tough": Heilemann and Halperin, *Game Change*.

"Elizabeth Warren, I could enjoy": Reid J. Epstein and Peter Nicholas, "Top Iowa Democrats Slow to Rally around Hillary," *Wall Street Journal*, January 4, 2015, http://www.wsj.com/articles/top-iowa-democrats-slow-to-rally-around-hillary-clinton-1420418121.

PART III: A PANTSUIT-WEARING GLOBETROTTER

CHAPTER 8: THE PRAETORIAN GUARD

"like the capo di tutti i capi": Interview with a Foreign Service officer who requested anonymity.

As the *Wall Street Journal* reported: Laura Meckler, "Clinton's Staff Kept Tight Rein on Documents," *Wall Street Journal*, May 20, 2015, http://www.wsj.com/articles/hillary-clintons-state-department-staff-kept-tight-rein-on-records-1432081701.

"Important policy papers": Interview with a Foreign Service officer who requested anonymity.

"She clearly didn't think": Ibid.

Jarrett wouldn't let Hillary get a word in edgewise: Ibid.

And she did a wicked impersonation of Bill Clinton: Ibid.

CHAPTER 9: SHAFTED

"I've been at State since the mid-1980s": Interview with a Foreign Service officer who requested anonymity.

"I don't want to be a pantsuit-wearing globetrotter": Interview with a Hillary Clinton friend who requested anonymity.

In her confrontations with Hillary: Susan B. Glasser, "Was Hillary Clinton a Good Secretary of State?," *Politico* magazine, December 8, 2013, http://www.politico.com/magazine/story/2013/12/was-hillary-clinton-a-good-secretary-of-state-john-kerry-2016-100766.html.

He defined her role: Glenn Thrush, "John Kerry: The Un–Hillary Clinton," *Politico*, February 21, 2013, http://www.politico.com/story/2013/02/john-kerry-the-un-hillary-clinton-87891.html.

"Don't expect to get your real marching orders": Edward Klein, *Blood Feud* (Washington, DC: Regnery Publishing, 2014).

CHAPTER 10: DOUBLE DIPPING

"extensive ties to the Muslim Brotherhood": Frank J. Gaffney Jr., "Huma Abedin's Private Emails, Muslim Brotherhood," *Washington Times*, March 6, 2015, https://news.brown.edu/articles/2013/03/warcosts.

"For all intents and purposes": Annie Karni, "Hillary's Shadow," *Politico*, July 2, 2015, http://www.politico.com/story/2015/07/hillary-clinton-2016-campaign-huma-abedin-119671.html.

CHAPTER 11: "I LOVE YOU, BILLY"

Their conversation took place: Interview with a State Department aide who requested anonymity.

CHAPTER 12: TOP TEN

"The Washington consensus": Susan B. Glasser, "Was Hillary Clinton a Good Secretary of State?," *Politico*, December 8, 2013, http://www.politico.com/magazine/story/2013/12/was-hillary-clinton-a-good-secretary-of-state-john-kerry-2016-100766.html.

I refused to put Boko Haram on a list: Adam Nossiter, "Boko Haram Militants Raped Hundreds of Female Captives in Nigeria," *New York Times*, May 18, 2015, http://www.nytimes.com/2015/05/19/world/africa/boko-haram-militants-raped-hundreds-of-female-captives-in-nigeria.html.

I received a report: Jeff Gerth and Sam Biddle, "Private Emails Reveal Ex-Clinton Aide's Secret Spy Network," ProPublica and Gawker, March 27, 2015, https://www.propublica.org/article/private-emails-reveal-ex-clinton-aides-secret-spy-network.

PART IV: THE FLOODGATES OPEN

CHAPTER 13: "GET CAUGHT TRYING"

Chelsea's overbearing, I-know-better attitude: Richard Johnson, "Staff Quit Clinton Foundation over Chelsea," *New York Post*, May 18, 2015.

IAC/InterActive paid Chelsea $50,000 a year: Amy Chozick, "Chelsea Clinton to Leave Well-Paid NBC News Job," *New York Times*, August 29, 2014, http://www.nytimes.com/2014/08/30/us/politics/chelsea-clinton-to-leave-nbc-news.html.

Business Insider calculated: Hunter Walker, "It Looks Like Chelsea Clinton Made $26,724 for Each Minute She Appeared on NBC," Business Insider, June 13, 2014, http://www.businessinsider.com/it-looks-like-chelsea-clinton-made-26724-for-each-minute-she-appeared-on-nbc-2014-6.

"[Chelsea's assignment] raises the obvious question": Michael Hiltzik, "Why Did NBC Reportedly Pay Chelsea Clinton $600,000 a Year?," *Los Angeles Times*, June 16, 2014, http://www.latimes.com/business/hiltzik/la-fi-mh-why-did-nbc-pay-chelsea-clinton-20140616-column.html#page=1.

"The Clinton Foundation [has] become a sprawling": Nicholas Confessore and Amy Chozick, "Unease at Clinton Foundation over Finances and Ambitions," *New York Times*, August 13, 2013, http://www.nytimes.com/2013/08/14/us/politics/unease-at-clinton-foundation-over-finances-and-ambitions.html.

"Inexcusable incompetence!": Interview with a close Clinton friend who requested anonymity.

"Whenever Hillary gave Bill holy hell": Interview with a source who spoke directly with Hillary.

"Bill was so rocked by their attack": Ibid.

Not long afterward, Chelsea got her wish: Isabel Vincent and Melissa Klein, "The Insider Who Opened the Door for Bill," *New York Post*, June 21, 2015.

It was a saying: Heather Wilhelm, "The Clinton Family's Telling Mantra," RealClearPolitics, May 28, 2015, http://www.real clearpolitics.com/articles/2015/05/28/clinton_familys_telling_ mantra_126753.html.

"Since marrying Chelsea": Matthew Goldstein and Steve Eder, "For Clintons, a Hedge Fund in the Family," *New York Times*, March 22, 2015, http://www.nytimes.com/2015/03/23/business/ dealbook/for-clintons-a-hedge-fund-in-the-family.html.

"Bill and Hillary were never enthusiastic": Interview with a close Clinton family friend who requested anonymity.

"Rock Creek Group": Goldstein and Eder, "For Clintons, a Hedge Fund."

He lost his shirt: Ibid.

"Investing in Greece is stupid": Author's interview with Larry Kudlow, March 26, 2015.

CHAPTER 14: IMAGINING "HILLARY 5.0"

"It is easy to forget": Amy Chozick, "Campaign Casts Hillary as the Populist It Insists She Has Always Been," *New York Times*, April 21, 2015, http://www.nytimes.com/2015/04/22/us/politics/hillary-clintons-quest-to-prove-her-populist-edge-is-as-strong-as-elizabeth-warrens.html.

"For more than a decade": Maggie Haberman, "Could Another Democrat Beat Hillary Clinton? Strategists Offer a Blueprint," *New York Times*, March 31, 2015, http://www.nytimes.com/2015/04/01/ us/politics/could-another-democrat-beat-hillary-clinton-strategists-offer-a-blueprint.

"Given that [Hillary] has been in public life": Nia-Malika Henderson, "Hillary Clinton Has Made Millions on Speeches. But She's Still Not a Great Speaker," *Washington Post*, December 9, 2014, http://www.washingtonpost.com/news/the-fix/wp/2014/12/09/hillary-clinton-has-made-millions-on-speeches-but-shes-still-not-a-great-speaker/.

"Her speaking style hasn't improved": Sean Trende, "Why Clinton's Emails Matter," RealClearPolitics, March 11, 2015, http://www.realclearpolitics.com/articles/2015/03/11/why_clintons_emails_matter_125899.html.

"I decided I had enough with the camera": Interview with a Clinton friend who requested anonymity.

"People familiar with Clinton's preparations": Philip Rucker and Anne Gearan, "The Making of Hillary 5.0: Marketing Wizards Help Reimagine Clinton Brand," *Washington Post*, February 21, 2015, http://www.washingtonpost.com/politics/the-making-of-hillary-50-marketing-wizards-help-reimagine-clinton-brand/2015/02/21/bfb01120-b919-11e4-aa05-1ce812b3fdd2_story.html.

"I'm just not entirely sure": Darren Samuelsohn, "Design Experts Trash Hillary Clinton's New Logo," *Politico*, April 17, 2015, http://www.politico.com/story/2015/04/design-experts-trash-hillary-clintons-new-logo-117100.html.

Kristina Schake, Michelle Obama's former communications chief: Amy Chozick, "This Woman's Job Is to Recast Hillary Clinton's Image," *New York Times*, April 3, 2015, http://www.nytimes.com/2015/04/05/style/this-woman-is-in-charge-of-shaping-hillary-clintons-image.html.

"A reputation for disingenuousness": Elizabeth Kolbert, "The Student," *New Yorker*, October 13, 2003, http://www.newyorker.com/magazine/2003/10/13/the-student.

CHAPTER 15: WOULDA, COULDA, SHOULDA

"The same time everybody else learned it": "President Obama with CBS News' Bill Plante: The Full Interview," CBS News, March 8, 2015, http://www.cbsnews.com/videos/president-obama-with-cbs-news-bill-plante-the-full-interview/.

That was the same answer: Sharyl Attkisson, "8 Times Obama Says He Was Way Out of the Loop," SharylAttkisson.com, March 9, 2015, https://sharylattkisson.com/8-times-obama-says-he-was-way-out-of-the-loop/.

"The White House explicitly warned Hillary": Interview with White House source who spoke with Valerie Jarrett and requested anonymity.

"That I don't know": Andrew Kirell, "Valerie Jarrett: 'I Don't Know' If Obama Officials Ever Received Emails from Hillary," Mediaite, March 6, 2015, http://www.mediaite.com/tv/valerie-jarrett-i-dont-know-if-obama-admin-officials-ever-received-emails-from-hillary/.

"thug": Interview with a source close to Valerie Jarrett who spoke on the condition of anonymity.

Now, Jarrett said, pacing the floor: Ibid.

"As much as I've been investigated": Andrew Kaczynski, "In 2000 Video Hillary Clinton Says She Doesn't 'Do Email' Because of Investigations into Her," BuzzFeed, March 4, 2015, http://www.buzzfeed.com/andrewkaczynski/watch-an-old-home-movie-from-2000-where-hillary-clinton-said#.bsxykW2kpG.

"It is the department's general policy": Jonathan Karl, "Hillary Clinton Was in Violation of State Dept. Policy for Nearly 6 Years," ABC World News, March 5, 2015, http://abcnews.go.com/Politics/hillary-clinton-violation-state-dept-policy-years/story?id=29424270.

"Based upon my first-hand involvement": Bob Cusack and Molly K. Hooper, "The Hillary Backer Who Will Pose Problems for Her 2016 bid," *Hill*, March 26, 2015, http://thehill.com/homenews/campaign/237012-the-backer-who-could-hurt-hillary.

"Her admitted destruction": Ronald D. Rotunda, "Hillary's Emails and the Law," *Wall Street Journal*, March 16, 2015, http://www.wsj.com/articles/ronald-d-rotunda-hillarys-emails-and-the-law-1426547356.

"Lack of speed kills in this case": Adam Edelman, "'Lack of Speed Kills in This Case': Former Obama Adviser Axelrod Blasts Clinton Team for Not Responding Better to Email Allegations," *New York Daily News*, March 5, 2015, http://www.nydailynews.com/news/politics/axelrod-rips-clinton-weak-response-email-allegations-article-1.2138537.

But Hillary hadn't given a political press conference: Glenn Thrush and Gabriel Debenedetti, "Hillary Clinton: I Used Private Email Account for 'Convenience,'" *Politico*, March 10, 2015, http://www.politico.com/story/2015/03/hillary-clinton-email-press-conference-115947.html.

The legal "review did not involve": Conor Friedersdorf, "Hillary Clinton's Questionable Process for Sorting Work Emails," *Atlantic*, March 13, 2015, http://www.theatlantic.com/politics/archive/2015/03/hillary-clintons-laughable-process-for-flagging-work-emails/387670/.

"The idea that such a process": Ibid.

"When Hillary first approached the podium": Ashe Schow, "Hillary Clinton Just Isn't That Likable," *Washington Examiner*, March 12, 2015, http://www.washingtonexaminer.com/hillary-clinton-just-isnt-that-likable/article/2561405.

"was an unmistakable message": John F. Harris, "Go to Hell," *Politico*, March 10 2015, http://www.politico.com/magazine/story/2015/03/hillary-clinton-press-conference-115958.html#.VcDzSJNViko.

"**Clinton put on a clinic**": Rem Rieder, "Rieder: The Lessons of Hillary's Press Debacle," *USA Today*, March 11, 2015, http://www.usatoday.com/story/money/columnist/rieder/2015/03/11/lessons-of-clinton-press-debacle/70141582/.

CHAPTER 16: "SKIN IN THE GAME"

There were several problems with this cozy arrangement: Nicholas Confessore and Michael S. Schmidt, "Clinton Friend's Memos on Libya Draw Scrutiny to Politics and Business," *New York Times*, May 18, 2015, http://www.nytimes.com/2015/05/19/us/politics/clinton-friends-libya-role-blurs-lines-of-politics-and-business.html.

Blumenthal worked for two companies: Michael S. Schmidt,"What Sidney Blumenthal's Memos to Hillary Clinton Said, and How They Were Handled," *New York Times*, May 18, 2015, http://www.nytimes.com/2015/05/19/us/politics/what-sidney-blumenthals-memos-to-hillary-clinton-said-and-how-they-were-handled.html.

"**encapsulates everything wrong**": Rich Lowry, "Sidney Blumenthal, the Clinton Foundation at Work," *National Review*, May 19, 2015, http://www.nationalreview.com/corner/418602/sidney-blumenthal-clinton-foundation-work-rich-lowry.

Hillary lied when she said: Edward Klein, *Blood Feud* (Washington, DC: Regnery Publishing, 2014).

As for McAuliffe: Kenric Ward, "Ties That Bind: Following the McAuliffe-Clinton Money Trail," Watchdog.org, October 29, 2013, http://watchdog.org/113331/clinton-mcauliffe/.

According to a report by the inspector general: Steve Eder, "Tony Rodham's Ties Invite Scrutiny for Hillary and Bill Clinton," *New York Times*, May 10, 2015, http://www.nytimes.com/2015/05/11/us/politics/tony-rodhams-ties-invite-scrutiny-forhillary-and-bill-clinton.html.

"the governor of Haiti": Garry Pierre-Pierre, "Our Man in Haiti: Bill Clinton," *Americas Quarterly*, Fall 2009, http://www.americas quarterly.org/garry-pierre-pierre-haiti.

"The two agencies in the world": Philip Rucker, "Haiti Holds a Special Place in the Hearts of Bill and Hillary Clinton," *Washington Post*, January 16, 2010, http://www.washingtonpost.com/wp-dyn/content/article/2010/01/15/AR2010011503820.html.

"I deal through the Clinton Foundation": Eder, "Tony Rodham's Ties."

A one-time adviser to Sani Abacha: "Hillary Clinton's Culture of Corruption May Doom Her Candidacy," *Investor's Business Daily*, March 26, 2015, http://news.investors.com/ibd-editorials/032615-745365-hillary-clinton-tony-rodham-terry-mcauliffe.htm?p=2.

"He's not Boko Haram": Daniel Wiser, "Senator Highlights Clinton Ties to Nigerian Donor: Vitter Investigates Clinton's Reluctance to Designate Boko Haram as Terrorist Group," Washington Free Beacon, March 25, 2015, http://freebeacon.com/national-security/senator-highlights-clinton-ties-to-nigerian-donor/.

In return for the favor: Peter Schweizer, *Clinton Cash: The Untold Story of How and Why Foreign Governments and Businesses Helped Make Bill and Hillary Rich* (New York: HarperCollins, 2015).

"As the Russians gradually assumed control": Jo Becker and Mike McIntire, "The Clintons, the Russians and Uranium," *New York Times*, April 24, 2015.

The donations were routed: Sean Davis, "Is the Clinton Foundation Just an International Money Laundering Scheme?," Federalist, April 29, 2915, http://thefederalist.com/2015/04/29/is-the-clinton-foundation-just-an-international-money-laundering-scheme/.

The news was a political bombshell: Joshua Green and Richard Rubin, "Clinton Foundation Failed to Disclose 1,100 Foreign Donations," Bloomberg Politics, April 29, 2015, http://www.

bloomberg.com/politics/articles/2015-04-29/clinton-foundation-failed-to-disclose-1-100-foreign-donations.

"Rather than taking cash": Davis, "Is the Clinton Foundation Just an International Money Laundering Scheme?"

The Charity Navigator: Gabriel Sherman, "The Clinton Foundation's behind-the-Scenes Battle with a Charity Watchdog Group," *New York* magazine, May 10, 2015, http://nymag.com/daily/intellig encer/2015/05/clinton-foundation-vs-a-charity-watchdog.html.

"I wonder if any aspirant for the presidency": Peggy Noonan, "How the Clintons Get Away with It," *Wall Street Journal*, May 9, 2015, http://www.wsj.com/articles/how-the-clintons-get-away-with-it-1431035304.

Qatar's winning committee suddenly ponied up: Jackie Kucinich, "Corrupt FIFA Has Clinton Foundation Ties; World Cup Host Qatar Gave Millions," Daily Beast, May 27, 2015, http://www.thedailybeast.com/articles/2015/05/27/corrupt-fifa-has-clinton-foundation-ties-world-cup-host-qatar-gave-millions.html.

The story of Hillary's dodgy behavior: Kimberley A. Strassel, "Hillary's Friends in High Places," *Wall Street Journal*, July 30, 2015, http://www.wsj.com/articles/hillarys-friends-in-high-places-1438301383.

"It never seems to end": Tom Bevan, "Will Steady Drip of Foundation Stories Soak Clinton?," RealClearPolitics, May 29, 2015, http://www.realclearpolitics.com/articles/2015/05/29/will_steady_drip_of_foundation_stories_soak_clinton_126774.html.

CHAPTER 17: A "CLASSIC WASHINGTON OMELETTE"

"The Clintons have been sent off": Matt Latimer, "Scandals Only Make the Clintons Stronger," *Politico* magazine, June 7, 2015, http://www.politico.com/magazine/story/2015/06/scandals-clintons-stronger-2016-foundation-president-118683.html#.VcD6C5NViko.

The Clinton's battle-tested strategy was simple: Margaret Carlson, "Hillary's Battle-Tested Strategy of Boredom," *New York Post*, May 26, 2015.

"Republicans trying to turn the Benghazi attacks into a scandal": *Real Time with Bill Maher*, May 11, 2013.

"Hillary Clinton…is in a different position": Michael Barone, "Clinton Defenders Advance an Unpersuasive Argument," *Washington Examiner*, April 30, 2015, http://www.washingtonexaminer.com/clinton-defenders-advance-an-unpersuasive-argument/article/2563730.

According to a Quinnipiac poll: Quinnipiac University National poll, April 23, 2015.

"honest and trustworthy": Zeke J. Miller, "Clinton Faces Biggest Threat from Rubio and Paul in New Poll," *Time*, May 28, 2015, http://time.com/3899309/hillary-clinton-marco-rubio-rand-paul/.

Yet another poll: Lisa Lerer and Emily Swanson, "AP-GfK Poll: Doubts about Clinton's Honesty after Emails," Associated Press, May 1, 2015, http://ap-gfkpoll.com/uncategorized/ap-gfk-poll-doubts-about-clintons-honesty-after-emails.

In late July: Niall Stanage, "Dem Fears over Clinton's Strength Grow after New Poll," *Hill*, July 22, 2015, http://thehill.com/homenews/campaign/248907-dem-fears-over-clintons-strength-grow-after-new-poll.

"Up until now": Charlie Cook, "Is Clinton's Tide Shifting?," *National Journal*, July 27, 2015, http://www.nationaljournal.com/off-to-the-races/is-clinton-s-tide-shifting-20150727.

Going one step further: Gabriel Schoenfeld, "Hillary Clinton's Email Woes Will Worsen: Why She Could Still Be in Serious Jeopardy," *New York Daily News*, August 3, 2015, http://www.nydailynews.com/opinion/gabriel-schoenfeld-hillary-clinton-email-woes-worsen-article-1.2311178.

"We…see a pattern of financial transactions": Peter Schweizer, *Clinton Cash: The Untold Story of How and Why Foreign Governments and Businesses Helped Make Bill and Hillary Rich* (New York: HarperCollins, 2015).

"It is highly unlikely": Michael Hirsch, "Bill and Hillary's Excellent Adventure," *Politico* magazine, April 25, 2015, http://www. politico.com/magazine/story/2015/04/bill-hillary-clinton-state-dept-117336.html#.VcD6jpNViko.

CHAPTER 18: THE SMOLDERING GUN?

"I worked for Hillary": Interview with a State Department intern who requested anonymity.

"During her last year at the State Department": Interview with a veteran Foreign Service officer who requested anonymity.

"When she flew on her Air Force C-32": Interview with a Foreign Service officer who requested anonymity.

PART V: PICKING UP THE PIECES

CHAPTER 19: THE POLITICAL ANIMAL

"the best political animal that's ever been in American politics": Geoffrey Dickens, "Charlie Rose to Bill Clinton: You Are the 'Best Political Animal That's Ever Been,'" NewsBusters, Media Research Center, October 1, 2014, http://newsbusters.org/blogs/geoffrey-dickens/2014/10/01/charlie-rose-bill-clinton-you-are-best-political-animal-thats-ever.

"Toss them all in the fireplace": Interview with a Clinton source who requested anonymity.

Hillary asked a well-known New York plastic surgeon: Interview with a friend of Hillary's who requested anonymity.

"She had her cheeks lifted": Ibid.

"To be really good at [politics] you've gotta like people": Dickens, "Charlie Rose to Bill Clinton."

A WMUR Granite State Poll: Ben Kamisar, "Poll: Clinton Trails Bush, Paul and Rubio in NH," *Ballot Box* (blog), *Hill*, May 7, 2015, http://thehill.com/blogs/ballot-box/presidential-races/241414-poll-clinton-trails-bush-paul-and-rubio-in-nh.

Another University of New Hampshire poll: Aaron Blake, "Is Hillary Clinton 'Likable Enough'? And Does It Even Matter?," *Washington Post*, February 9, 2015, http://www.washingtonpost.com/news/the-fix/wp/2015/02/09/is-hillary-clinton-likable-enough-and-why-does-it-even-matter/.

That press conference: Jason Zengerle, "Is Hillary Clinton Any Good at Running for President?," *New York* magazine, April 5, 2015, http://nymag.com/daily/intelligencer/2015/04/hillary-clinton-2016-campaign.html.

"She's like Pete Rose": Ibid.

"Hillary still obsesses about money": Maureen Dowd, "When Will Hillary Let It Go?," *New York Times*, June 14, 2014, http://www.nytimes.com/2014/06/15/opinion/sunday/maureen-dowd-when-will-hillary-let-it-go.html.

"The presidency...isn't all that powerful": George Packer, "The Choice," *New Yorker*, January 28, 2008, http://www.newyorker.com/magazine/2008/01/28/the-choice-6.

"He'll show up at your birthday party": Interview with a close Clinton ally who requested anonymity.

CHAPTER 20: "WHEN YOU GOT IT, FLAUNT IT"

First,...you must protect your left flank: Interview with a guest at a Clinton dinner party who requested anonymity.

CHAPTER 21: DINNER WITH LIZ

Bill Clinton had a recurring nightmare: Interviews with several of Bill Clinton's friends, all of whom requested anonymity.

"I've heard from state committeemen": Ibid.

The Clintons flew in a private jet: Interviews with members of the Kennedy family who requested anonymity.

"Bill was in full campaign mode": Ibid.

A week after: Ibid.

"Liz said that she's flattered": Interview with a member of the Kennedy family who requested anonymity.

When the Clintons received word: Interviews with a number of Clinton confidants who requested anonymity.

PART VI: THE VENDETTA

CHAPTER 22: WHISPERING CAMPAIGN

"Val told me that the polls were rigged": Interview with a source close to Valerie Jarrett who requested anonymity.

"total fool": Nick Wing, "Bill Clinton: Obama Risks Looking Like a 'Wuss,' 'a Total Fool' If He Doesn't Act on Syria," Huffington Post, June 13, 2013, http://www.huffingtonpost.com/2013/06/13/bill-clinton-obama-syria_n_3434393.html.

"Great nations need organizing principles": Jeffrey Goldberg, "Hillary Clinton: 'Failure' to Help Syrian Rebels Led to the Rise of ISIS," *Atlantic*, August 10, 2014, http://www.theatlantic.com/international/archive/2014/08/hillary-clinton-failure-to-help-syrian-rebels-led-to-the-rise-of-isis/375832/.

"frat house": Dana Milbank, "Hillary Clinton Rebrands Obama's Frat House as Her Own," *Washington Post*, February 17, 2015, https://www.washingtonpost.com/opinions/hillary-clinton-rebrands-obamas-frat-house-as-her-own/2015/02/17/1d0ab0fc-b6e8-11e4-9423-f3d0a1ec335c_story.html.

"**[Hillary's people] are planning to hold off deciding**": Internal memo leaked to the author by a campaign aide working for a rival of Hillary's for the nomination.

"**The Clintons are consciously going out**": Ibid.

"**[Hillary] and the Obama White House really, really hated**": Glenn Thrush, "Nicole Wallace to Carly Fiorina: Hands Off Hillary," *Politico*, May 14, 2015, http://www.politico.com/story/2015/05/nicole-wallace-to-carly-fiorina-hands-off-hillary-117940.html.

linked the words "blood feud" directly to the "Democratic Party": Robert Draper, "The Great Democratic Crack-Up of 2016," *New York Times Magazine*, May 12, 2015, www.nytimes.com/2015/05/17/magazine/the-great-democratic-crack-up-of-2016.html.

"**Ideologically, it pitted so-called 'Elizabeth Warren Democrats'**": Ibid.

"**Mrs. Clinton's political operation**": Nicholas Confessore and Amy Chozick, "Emerging Clinton Team Shows Signs of Disquiet," *New York Times*, February 11, 2015, http://www.nytimes.com/2015/02/11/us/politics/emerging-clinton-team-shows-signs-of-disquiet.html.

"**It seems highly unlikely**": Author's interview with Henry Sheinkopf, January 3, 2014.

the e-mail scandal was timed by Jarrett to hit the headlines: Interview with someone who spoke directly to Valerie Jarrett and who requested anonymity.

six separate probes: Interview with State Department source who requested anonymity.

CHAPTER 23: ON THE QT

let Hillary know on the QT: Interview with State Department source and a source who spoked directly with Hillary Clinton. Both requested anonymity.

When Kerry was a senator: Darren Garnick and Ilya Mirman, "If the Walls Could Talk," Slate, October 28, 2010, http://www.slate.com/articles/news_and_politics/politics/2010/10/if_the_walls_could_talk.html.

"When Kerry made a comment in 2006": Matt Viser, "With Clinton E-mail Mess, Kerry Faces Balancing Act," *Boston Globe*, April 14, 2015, https://www.bostonglobe.com/news/politics/2015/04/14/john-kerry-faces-balancing-act-manages-hillary-clinton-email-mess-state-department/uTE8A9tK99zk3uw6Q8l50O/story.html.

"Kerry is focused on creating a legacy for himself": Ibid.

"My contacts and friends in newspapers and TV": Interview with anonymous source.

"She's grinding her teeth at night again": Interview with an anonymous Clinton source.

CHAPTER 24: SOMEBODY "O'MALLEABLE"

Obama's decision: Maggie Haberman, "Clinton: 'No Obama Immigration Action May Have Hurt in Midterms,'" *Politico*, November 15, 2014, http://www.politico.com/story/2014/11/clinton-no-obama-immigration-action-may-have-hurt-in-midterms-112924.html.

The meeting with Hillary: Interview with anonymous sources close to both Hillary and Valerie Jarrett.

"You must be busy": Ibid.

"After Hillary was gone": Interview with a source who spoke directly with Valerie Jarrett and who requested anonymity.

Valerie's search for an alternative: Ibid.

CHAPTER 25: A SUB ROSA INVESTIGATION

"We ate on the new White House china service": Interview with an anonymous source who dined with Valerie Jarrett and the Obamas in the White House.

"You need to do your duty": Ibid.

CHAPTER 26: MISSING IN ACTION

"According to people familiar with her thinking": Noah Rothman, "*NY Times*: Clinton's Conspicuous Absence at Selma Celebrations Did Not Go Unnoticed," *Hot Air* (blog), March 90, 2015, http://hotair.com/archives/2015/03/09/ny-times-clintons-conspicuous-absence-at-selma-celebrations-did-not-go-unnoticed/.

"Hillary would have even gone alone": Interview with an anonymous Clinton source.

For the privilege of hosting: Geoff Earle, "Students Get Billed," *New York Post*, June 1, 2015.

"As usual, women were all over Bill": Interview with anonymous source who attended the South Beach fund-raiser with Bill Clinton.

CHAPTER 27: A TABLOID STAPLE

As Hillary later described the scene to friends: Interviews with sources close to Hillary, who spoke on the condition of anonymity about her fight with Bill in January 2015.

Ghislaine would later be accused: Anna Pukas, "Revealed: The Woman at the Centre of the Prince Andrew Scandal … Ghislaine Maxwell," *London Express*, updated January 26, 2015, http://www.express.co.uk/news/royal/550433/Ghislaine-Maxwell-Prince-Andrew-sex-abuse-scandal.

"What [originally] attracted Clinton to Epstein": Landon Thomas Jr., "Jeffrey Epstein: International Moneyman of Mystery," *New York* magazine, October 28, 2002, http://nymag.com/nymetro/news/people/n_7912/.

"I only ever met Bill twice": Sharon Churcher and Polly Dunbar, "Teenage Girl Recruited by Paedophile Jeffrey Epstein Reveals How She Twice Met Bill Clinton," *Daily Mail* (UK), March 5, 2011, http://www.dailymail.co.uk/news/article-1363452/Bill-Clinton-15-year-old-masseuse-I-met-twice-claims-Epsteins-girl.html.

The reckless billionaire: Vicky Ward, "I Tried to Warn You about Sleazy Billionaire Jeffrey Epstein in 2003," Daily Beast, January 6, 2015, http://www.thedailybeast.com/articles/2015/01/06/i-tried-to-warn-you-about-sleazy-billionaire-jeffrey-epstein-in-2002.html.

I interviewed Epstein by telephone: Edward Klein, "The Trouble with Andrew," *Vanity Fair*, August 2011, http://www.vanityfair.com/news/2011/08/prince-andrew-201108.

"Bill's Libido Threatens to Derail Hillary—Again": Maureen Callahan, "Bill's Libido Threatens to Derail Hillary—Again," *New York Post*, February 14, 2015, http://www.vanityfair.com/news/2011/08/prince-andrew-201108.

"Bill was sipping iced tea": Interview with a Clinton legal adviser who requested anonymity.

PART VII: SHAMELESS

CHAPTER 28: THE POTEMKIN CAMPAIGN

In recent years: Taegan Goddard's Political Dictionary, http://political dictionary.com/.

"Her aides are planning a different sort of campaign": Peter Nicholas, "Clinton Campaign's Challenge: Make Her 'Likable,'" *Washington Wire* (blog), *Wall Street Journal*, April 12, 2015, http://blogs.wsj.com/washwire/2015/04/12/clinton-campaigns-challenge-make-her-likeable/.

that came to one question every 3.6 days: Chris Cillizza, "Hillary Clinton Hasn't Answered a Question from the Media in 20 Days," *Washington Post*, May 11, 2015, http://www.washingtonpost.com/news/the-fix/wp/2015/05/11/hillary-clinton-hasnt-answered-a-question-from-the-media-in-20-days/.

"This is exactly what I want to do": Tamara Keith, "The 13 Questions Hillary Clinton Has Answered from the Press," National Public Radio, May 13, 2015, http://www.npr.org/sections/itsallpolitics/2015/05/13/406250488/the-13-questions-hillary-clinton-has-answered-from-the-press.

"Who would be able to raise money": Julie Pace, "If Clinton Is Elected, Family Foundation Could Face Changes," Associated Press, May 11, 2015.

"This is the first installment": Amy Chozick, "Questions for Hillary Clinton: Immigration," *FirstDraft* (blog), *New York Times*, May 6, 2015, http://www.nytimes.com/politics/first-draft/2015/05/06/questions-for-hillary-clinton-immigration/.

It posted an online clock: Philip Bump, "Here's a Clock That Counts the Minutes Since Hillary Clinton Answered a Press Question," *Washington Post*, May 12, 2015, http://www.washingtonpost.com/news/the-fix/wp/2015/05/12/heres-a-clock-that-counts-the-minutes-since-hillary-clinton-answered-a-press-question/.

In her first thirty days: Annie Linskey, "N.H. Voters Take Lack of Access to Clinton Personally," *Boston Globe*, May 20, 2015, https://www.bostonglobe.com/news/nation/2015/05/19/hillary-clinton-campaign-stays-arms-length-from-everyday-voters/42GU5L0KX3UYxKYqNj6iJM/story.html.

She appeared at sixteen fund-raisers: Jennifer Epstein, "Manhattan Moguls, including Beyonce, Turn Out for Hillary Clinton," Bloomberg Politics, May 13, 2015, http://www.bloomberg.com/politics/articles/2015-05-13/from-listening-tour-to-fundraising-frenzy-manhattan-moguls-embrace-hillary-clinton.

"The reality is that Clinton's avoidance": Josh Kraushaar, "Hillary Clinton's Quiet Self-Sabotage," *National Journal*, May 26, 2015, http://www.nationaljournal.com/against-the-grain/hillary-clinton-s-quiet-self-sabotage-20150526.

At a campaign event in Cedar Falls: Gabriel Debenedetti, "Fundraiser Puts Spotlight on Clinton Foundation Finances," *Politico*, May 20, 2015, http://www.politico.com/story/2015/05/fundraiser-clinton-foundation-finances-118128.html.

"Spectacle of Clinton as candidate": Tweet from Maggie Haberman @maggieNYT, July 4, 2015, https://twitter.com/maggienyt/status/617399718239412224.

"Hang 'em high, Hillary": Roger Simon, "Hillary Rope-a-Dopes Press, but Who's the Dope?," *Politico*, July 7, 2015, http://www.politico.com/story/2015/07/roger-simon-hillary-clinton-press-119777.html.

To Goodwin's ear: Michael Goodwin, "Two-Faced Hill Razer," *New York Post*, May 20, 2015.

CHAPTER 29: ON THE "PRECARIOUS LEFT EDGE"

"Hillary has kept Bill on the sidelines": Interview with a Clinton confidant who requested anonymity.

Bill told his advisers: Interview with anonymous sources who spoke directly with Bill Clinton.

"If his advice is asked for": Ben Kamisar, "Bill Won't Campaign for Hillary in 2015, Aides Say," *Ballot Box* (blog), *Hill*, May 11, 2015, http://thehill.com/blogs/ballot-box/presidential-races/241605-bill-wont-campaign-for-hillary-in-2015-aides-say.

"Hillary Rodham Clinton is running the most liberal": Anne Gearan, "Clinton Is Banking on the Obama Coalition to Win," *Washington Post*, May 17, 2015, http://www.washingtonpost.com/politics/running-to-the-left-hillary-clinton-is-banking-on-the-obama-coalition-to-win/2015/05/17/33b7844a-fb28-11e4-9ef4-1bb7ce3b3fb7_story.html.

CHAPTER 30: "A HYDRA-HEADED BEAST"

they were worried sick: This chapter is based on a series of interviews with an anonymous source who spoke on several occasions with

Hillary and Bill Clinton about how the 2016 election campaign impacted their family.

CHAPTER 31: "IT'S GONE WAY TOO FAR"

Barack Obama could hardly contain his excitement: This chapter is based on a series of interviews with sources who spoke directly with Valerie Jarrett about her discussions with the president and Mrs. Obama regarding Hillary Clinton.

EPILOGUE: THAT OLD CAR SMELL

"Has American culture become gross": Stan Latreille, "An Old Fogey Sounds Off on Coarsening of Language, Dress, Music, Manners," Livingston Post, December 9, 2013, http://thelivingstonpost.com/ an-old-fogey-sounds-off-on-coarsening-of-language-dress-music- and-manners/.

"I am glad that I'm not raising kids today": Nick Gillespie, "Society Is Coarser—but Better," *Time*, October 9, 2013, http://ideas.time. com/2013/10/09/yes-society-is-coarser-and-better/. Emphasis in original.

"The cruel, perverse and obscene": Jacques Barzun, *From Dawn to Decadence* (New York: Harper Perennial, 2001).

"I think the American people": Zeke J. Miller, "Obama: Voters Want 'New Car Smell' in 2016," *Time*, November 23, 2014, http://time. com/3601329/obama-new-car-election-2016/.

"Nobody wants to go to a fund-raiser": Maureen Dowd, "Hooray for Hillarywood?," *New York Times*, May 30, 2015, http://www. nytimes.com/2015/05/31/opinion/sunday/maureen-dowd-hooray- for-hillarywood-hillary-clinton.html.

Her "favorability" with that cohort: Josh Kraushaar, "Hillary Clinton's Quiet Self-Sabotage," *National Journal*, May 26, 2015, http://www.nationaljournal.com/against-the-grain/hillary-clinton-s-quiet-self-sabotage-20150526.

"Warren has suggested": David Frum, "Run, Warren, Run," *Atlantic*, January 13, 2015.

"[Hillary] is so terrified of losing Iowa": Mark Halperin, "Hillary Clinton Is Terrified of the Left," Bloomberg Television, April 16, 2015, http://www.bloomberg.com/politics/videos/2015-04-16/mark-halperin-hillary-clinton-is-terrified-of-the-left.

"On the party's favorite issue of income inequality": Ed Rogers, "The Insiders: How Will Clinton Reconcile Her Past with Her Platform?," *Washington Post*, June 8, 2015, http://www.washingtonpost.com/blogs/post-partisan/wp/2015/06/08/the-insiders-how-will-clinton-reconcile-her-past-with-her-platform/.

Hillary's "magnitude of experience": Brent Budowsky, "The Magic of Bill Clinton," *Hill*, May 20, 2015, http://thehill.com/opinion/brent-budowsky/242732-brent-budowsky-the-magic-of-bill-clinton.

"Becoming the first female president": Richard Cohen, "Just Being Hillary Clinton Isn't Enough," *Washington Post*, August 12, 2013, https://www.washingtonpost.com/opinions/richard-cohen-just-being-hillary-clinton-isnt-enough/2013/08/12/3734074c-037c-11e3-a07f-49ddc7417125_story.html.

SELECTED BIBLIOGRAPHY

Alinsky, Saul D. *Rules for Radicals: A Pragmatic Primer for Realistic Radicals*. New York: Vintage Books, 1989. Originally published 1971, Random House, New York.

Allen, Jonathan, and Amie Parnes. *HRC: State Secrets and the Rebirth of Hillary Clinton*. New York: Crown Publishers, 2014.

Barzun, Jacques. *From Dawn to Decadence: 500 Years of Western Cultural Life, 1500 to the Present*. New York: Harper Perennial, 2001.

Bernstein, Carl. *A Woman in Charge*. New York: Alfred A. Knopf, 2007.

Bozell, L. Brent, III, with Tim Graham. *Whitewash: What the Media Won't Tell You about Hillary Clinton, but Conservatives Will*. New York: Crown Forum, 2007.

Brimelow, Peter. *The Worm in the Apple: How the Teacher Unions Are Destroying American Education*. New York: HarperCollins, 2003.

Califano, Joseph A., Jr. *The Triumph & Tragedy of Lyndon Johnson: The White House Years*. New York: Touchstone, 1991.

Chafe, William H. *Bill and Hillary: The Politics of the Personal*. New York: Farrar, Straus and Giroux, 2012.

Coulter, Ann. *Demonic: How the Liberal Mob Is Endangering America*. New York: Crown Forum, 2011.

Dallek, Robert. *Hail to the Chief: The Making and Unmaking of American Presidents*. New York: Hyperion, 1996.

Gates, Robert M. *Duty: Memoirs of a Secretary at War*. New York: Alfred A. Knopf, 2014.

Gibbs, Nancy, and Michael Duffy. *The Presidents Club: Inside the World's Most Exclusive Fraternity*. New York: Simon & Schuster, 2012.

Greenhut, Steven. *Plunder! How Public Employee Unions Are Raiding Treasuries, Controlling Our Lives and Bankrupting the Nation*. California: Forum Press, 2009.

Greenstein, Fred I. *The Presidential Difference: Leadership Style from FDR to Barack Obama*. 3rd ed. Princeton: Princeton University Press, 2009.

Halper, Daniel. *Clinton Inc.: The Audacious Rebuilding of a Political Machine*. New York: Broadside, 2014.

Halperin, Mark, and John Heilemann. *Double Down: Game Change 2012*. New York: Penguin Press, 2013.

Harris, John F. *The Survivor: Bill Clinton in the White House*. New York: Random House, 2005.

Hedtke, James R. *Lame Duck Presidents—Myth or Reality*. New York: Edwin Mellen Press, 2002.

Heilemann, John, and Mark Halperin. *Game Change: Obama and the Clintons, McCain and Palin, and the Race of a Lifetime*. New York: HarperCollins, 2010.

Horowitz, David, and Jacob Laksin. *The New Leviathan: How the Left-Wing Money Machine Shapes American Politics and Threatens America's Future*. New York: Crown Forum, 2012.

Horowitz, David, and Richard Poe. *The Shadow Party: How George Soros, Hillary Clinton, and Sixties Radicals Seized Control of the Democratic Party*. Nashville: Thomas Nelson, 2006.

Kantor, Jodi. *The Obamas*. New York: Little, Brown and Company, 2012.

Kirk, Russell. *The Conservative Mind*. California: BN Publishing, 2008.

Malanga, Steven. *The New New Left: How American Politics Works Today*. Chicago: Ivan R. Dee, 2005.

Mendell, David. *Obama: From Promise to Power*. New York: Amistad, 2007.

Morris, Dick, and Eileen McGann. *Power Grab: Obama's Dangerous Plan for a One Party Nation*. Florida: Humanix Books, 2014.

Nasr, Vali. *The Dispensable Nation: American Foreign Policy in Retreat*. New York: Doubleday, 2013.

Neustadt, Richard E. *Presidential Power and the Modern Presidents*. New York: Free Press, 1990.

Noonan, Peggy. *The Case against Hillary Clinton*. New York: ReganBooks, 2000.

Olson, Barbara. *Hell to Pay: The Unfolding Story of Hillary Rodham Clinton*. Washington, DC: Regnery Publishing, 1999.

Oppenheimer, Jerry. *State of a Union: Inside the Complex Marriage of Bill and Hillary Clinton*. New York: HarperCollins Publishers, 2000.

Ringer, Robert. *Restoring the American Dream: The Defining Voice in the Movement for Liberty*. Hoboken: John Wiley & Sons, 2010.

Segur, Philippe-Paul de. *Napoleon's Russian Campaign*. Boston: Houghton Mifflin Company / The Riverside Press Cambridge, 1958.

Siegel, Fred. *The Revolt against the Masses: How Liberalism Has Undermined the Middle Class*. New York: Encounter Books, 2013.

Smith, Sally Bedell. *For Love of Politics: Bill and Hillary Clinton; The White House Years*. New York: Random House, 2007.

Stephens, Bret. *America in Retreat: The New Isolationism and the Coming Global Disorder*. New York: Sentinel, 2014.

Storr, Anthony. *Feet of Clay: Saints, Sinners, and Madmen; A Study of Gurus*. New York: Free Press, 1996.

Tomasky, Michael. *Hillary's Turn: Inside Her Improbable, Victorious Senate Campaign*. New York: Free Press, 2001.

Willey, Kathleen. *Target: Caught in the Crosshairs of Bill and Hillary Clinton*. Los Angeles: World Ahead Publishing Company, 2007.

Wolffe, Richard. *The Message: The Reselling of President Obama*. New York: Twelve, Hachette Book Group, 2013.

Woodward, Bob. *The Price of Politics*. New York: Simon & Schuster, 2012.

York, Byron. *The Vast Left Wing Conspiracy: The Untold Story of the Democrats' Desperate Fight to Reclaim Power*. New York: Three Rivers Press, 2005.

INDEX

A

Abacha, Sani, 126
Abedin, Huma, 24, 66, 72, 81, 97,
    115, 122, 140–41, 182, 212
    background of, 77–78
    double dipping, 79–80
Affleck, Ben, 160
AFL-CIO, 157
African Americans, 24–25, 52, 93, 156
Alinsky, Saul, 102
Allen, Woody, 199
Almanac of American Presidents, The
    (Barone), 134
al Qaeda, 78, 122–23, 125
Amanpour, Christiane, 213

America, 16–18, 21, 77, 122, 128,
    160, 208
    coarsening of, 228–30
    culture of, 51, 227–28
    foreign policy of, 74, 86, 134, 151, 213
    money to Haiti, 124
    politics in, 52, 55–56, 117, 119,
        129, 134, 147, 149, 162, 174,
        212–15, 227–28, 235–37
American Bridge PAC, 120
Andrew, Prince, 198–200
Ansar al-Sharia, 122
Asia, 82, 86, 142, 215
Associated Press, 135, 207
Atlantic, the, 115, 169, 234
Avenue Capital, 98
Axelrod, David, 74, 113

B

Baltimore, MD, 24–25
Band, Doug, 73, 79, 93–95, 197
Barbara Lee Family Foundation, 9
Bardack, Lisa, 30
Barone, Michael, 134
Barzun, Jacques, 230
Begala, John, 24, 32, 142
Beijing, 77, 82, 86, 198
Benenson, Joel, 170
Benghazi, 120, 178
  e-mails about, 87, 123
  as a Hillary scandal, 23, 134, 236
  known to be dangerous, 87, 121–22
  "What difference does it make?,"
    43, 151
Bergdahl, Bowe, 151
Bernstein, Carl, 42
Beschloss, Afsaneh, 99
Bevan, Tom, 131
Biden, Beau, 185
Biden, Joseph "Joe," 109, 185
  death of son, 185
  as possible challenger to Hillary,
    109, 185, 225–26
Bill, Hillary & Chelsea Clinton Foun-
  dation, 17, 92. *See also* Clinton
  Foundation
Bill and Hillary Clinton National Air-
  port, 12
billionaires, 17, 12, 125, 197, 199, 209
Bird, Jeremy, 170
Blair, Diane, 47
Blankfein, Lloyd C., 98
Blood Feud (Klein), 120–22, 150,
  172–73
"Bloody Sunday," 191
Blumenthal, Sidney, xi–xiii, 87, 110–
  11, 119–20, 122

Boko Haram, 86, 125–26
Boston Globe, 178–79
Broaddrick, Juanita, 200
Browning, Dolly Kyle, 200
Buchanan, Pat, 151
Bush, George W., 61, 133, 143, 191,
  214, 231, 234
Bush, Jeb, 136, 150, 158, 221

C

Canada, 128
Cancro, Robert, 41
Caputo, Lisa, 46–47
Carter, Jimmy, 174, 215
Carville, James, 24, 32, 142
Cayne, James "Jimmy," 199
CBS News, 107
Cedar Falls, IA, 209
Chafee, Lincoln, 109, 184, 232–33
Chagoury, Gilbert, 126
Chappaqua, NY, 12, 23–24, 31–32,
  93, 98, 112, 115, 148, 155, 175, 196
Cher, 160
Chinagate, 109
Chipotle, 212
Chozick, Amy, 207
Cillizza, Chris, 205–6
Citizens United, 215
Clark, Wendy, 104
Clinton, Chelsea, 79, 98, 155
  Clinton Foundation and, 17, 20,
    91–95, 193, 219–20
  confrontation with Bill over foun-
    dation, 93–95
  "get caught trying" slip, 96
  as likely first lady to Hillary, 20
  NBC job, 92, 94
  relationship with parents, 32, 95,
    219–20

speaking fees, 17

temper, 8, 94, 96

wedding, 97, 115, 198

Clinton, Hillary Rodham

absent from Selma event, 191–93

agreement with Obama White
House, xii–xiii, 73, 111

anger issues, 42–43, 72, 195–96

appearance of, 147–49

bipartisanship in Senate, 48–49

David Geffen and, 55–56

"dead broke" comment, 16, 123,
151

distancing from Obama, 215

e-mail scandal, 87, 107–117, 119–
21, 137–38, 175, 188, 220–21

FBI investigation of, 188–89, 220

feud with Obamas, 71–76, 109–11,
168–70, 172–75, 177–82, 188,
224–25

fights with Bill, xii, 10, 195–96

as first lady, 21

health, 28–32

as liar, 42, 56, 61

liberal credentials, 101–2

likeability lessons, 3–6, 102–3

makeovers, 45–49, 104–5

as misanthrope, 40–41

Oprah and, 51–54

paid speeches, 7–8, 17, 151–52

parents of, 38–40, 42

"personality deficit," 58

rebranding of, 104–5

reliance on Bill, 37–38, 91

scandals and, 23, 129, 133–35,
152, 236

as secretary of state, 65–69, 71–83,
85–87, 119–31, 137, 139–44,
151, 175

sees self as victim, xv–xvi

shamelessness, 21

as similar to Claire Underwood, 10

2008 campaign. *See* 2008 presidential primary

2016 campaign, 15, 23, 25, 80, 91,
133–37, 155–57, 184, 205–10,
218–20, 231–36

unlikeability of, 41, 49, 57, 61, 149–
51, 232

visit to Kennedy Compound, 160–
62

Clinton, William Jefferson "Bill"

absent from Selma event, 191–93

advice for Hillary, 3–4, 31, 72–73,
81–83, 143–44, 147–48, 155–
58, 214

agreement with Obama White
House, xii–xiii, 73, 111

David Geffen and, 55–56

dealings during Hillary's time at
State, 87, 119–31, 137, 140–41

excellent at politics, 152–53

feud with Obamas, xii, 109–11,
168–70, 172–75, 177–82, 188,
224–25

as first gentleman, 19–21

frequent conversations with Hillary,
10, 91

as governor, 7, 38

health, 25–28

impeachment, 66, 133–34, 236

Jeffrey Epstein and, 195–202

lifestyle of, 10–21, 82, 94–95

1992 presidential campaign, 24, 45

Oprah and, 52–53

out of loop on Hillary's campaign,
211–13

paid speeches, 7–8, 15–16

pardons granted, 55–56
political infidelity of, 13–14, 27
popularity of, 16
relationship with Marc Mezvinsky,
    97–98
shamelessness, 21
as similar to Frank Underwood, 10
visit to Kennedy Compound, 160–62
Clinton administration, 53, 55, 75,
    102, 113, 156, 233–34
Clinton Cash (Schweizer), 126–27
Clinton Foundation, 17, 123, 198,
    209–10, 213
    as access to Clintons, 18
    agreement with Obama White
        House regarding, xiii, 73, 87
    control of, 32–34, 91–95, 219
    Donna Shalala and, 32–34, 193, 219
    Doug Band and, 93–95
    foreign donations to, xii–xiii, 73,
        110–11, 126–31, 188–89, 232
    Hillary's work for while at State,
        23, 125–26, 130, 135, 137, 139–
        44, 175, 189, 232
    Huma Abedin and, 79
    humanitarian work done by, 17–18,
        82, 116, 125
    importance to Bill, 14–16, 19,
        33–34
    Marc Mezvinsky and, 97–98
    media coverage of, xii, 15–16,
        92–93
    name change, 17, 91
    speaking fees transferred to, 17
    tax errors, 16
    Tony Rodham and, 23, 125
    2016 election and, 15, 18–19, 207
Clinton Giustra Enterprise Partner-
    ship, 128

Clinton Global Initiative, 12, 15, 18,
    98–99, 125, 142–43, 193
Clinton White House, 53, 61, 66, 78,
    95, 99, 156, 201
Colorado, 135–36, 158
conservatives, 78, 108, 136, 151, 167,
    192, 229–32
Cook, Charlie, 136
Cook Political Report, The, 136
Council Bluffs, IA, 209
Couric, Katie, 48, 199
Crimea, 86, 151
Cuba, 68
Cummings, Elijah, 24

D

Daily Mail, 198
Dalai Lama, the, 56
Danson, Ted, 97
Davis, Sean, 17, 128
de Blasio, Bill, 109
Democratic National Committee, 171,
    188, 217–18
Democratic National Convention, 21,
    60
Democratic Party, Democrats, 55, 59,
    79, 97–98, 101, 123, 135, 209, 214
    base of, 170, 184, 232–33
    Clintons' fight to control, 170, 172–
        74, 217–18, 221
    hard Left of, 18
    Kennedy family and, 161–62
    populist wing of, 101, 160, 173,
        235
    presidential elections and. *See spe-
        cific elections*
    presidential primaries and. *See spe-
        cific primaries*

view of Obama in 2014 elections,
167–68, 181
Dibble, Elizabeth, 122
Diller, Barry, 92
Domestic Policy Council, 53
Dowd, Maureen, 54–56, 152, 232
Draper, Robert, 172
DreamWorks SKG, 54
Duty (Gates), 49

E

Eaglevale, 97, 99
East Asia, 82
Edmund Pettus Bridge, 191–92
Edwards, John, 57
Emanuel, Rahm, 74
Epstein, Jeffrey, 97, 196–201
Ethiopia, 223

F

Federal Bureau of Investigation (FBI),
56, 188, 220–21
Federal Records Act, 113
Fédération Internationale de Football
Association (FIFA), 129
Filegate, 109
First Draft (blog), 207
Florida, 136, 158, 193, 199
Flowers, Gennifer, 200
Foggy Bottom, 65, 68, 73, 75, 86, 112,
126, 140, 175, 178. *See also* U.S.
Department of State
Foreign Service, 65, 67–68, 72, 141–42,
177
Foster, Vince, 109, 134
Fox, Nicole, 97
Fox News, 136, 209
Freedom of Information Act, 113

From Dawn to Decadence (Barzun),
230

G

Gaddafi, Muammar, 86
Gaffney, Frank, Jr., 78
Game Change, 8, 240
Gandhi, Mohandas, 41
Gates, Robert, 49
Gearan, Anne, 214
Geffen, David, 54–56
Georgetown University, 151, 164, 229
Gerth, Jeff, 41
Ghana, 197
Gibbs, Robert, 74
Giustra, Frank, 126–28
GOP, the, 171. *See also* Republican
Party, Republicans
Gorham, NH, 209
Gowdy, Trey, 120
Gracen, Elizabeth Ward, 200
#GrandmothersKnowBest, 9
"Great Democratic Crack-Up of 2016,
The" (Draper), 172
Greece, 99
Greenberg, Alan "Ace," 199
Greenberg, Stan, 45–46
GreenTech Automotive, 124
Gregory, Edgar, 55
Gregory, Vonna Jo, 55
Guiney, Timothy Edward, 27–28

H

Haberman, Maggie, 209
Haiti, 8, 12, 19–20, 124–25, 142–43
Halperin, Mark, 8, 234, 240
Hard Choices (Clinton), 149–50
Harris, John F., 117

Hart, Gary, 135
hdr2@clintonemail.com, 87, 114, 120
Heilemann, John, 8, 240
Henry, Ed, 209
Her Way (Gerth and Van Natta), 41
Hines, Cheryl, 162
Hispanics, 156, 158, 179, 181, 184, 228
Holbrooke, Richard, 67
Hollywood, 3, 5–6, 8, 54, 56, 160, 232
Home Improvement, 47
Homeland Security. *See* U.S. Department of Homeland Security
Hong Kong, 82, 197
Hot Air, 192
House of Cards, 10
HRod17@clintonemail.com, 120
Hudson Institute, 136

I

IAC/InterActiveCorp, 92
Investor's Business Daily, 126
Iowa, 7, 23, 49, 51, 56–58, 61, 135, 161, 179, 206, 209, 213, 218, 224, 234
Iran, 73, 116, 173, 179
"Is Clinton's Tide Shifting?" (Cook), 136
Islam, 78, 86, 122, 125, 151, 169, 178, 183
Islamic State, 86, 151, 169, 183
Israel, 67, 73, 173
It's Your World (Clinton), 96
It Takes a Village (Sheehan), 47

J

Jackson, Jesse, 14, 56
Japan, 74–75, 82

Jarrett, Valerie, 72, 167
closeness to Obama, xi, 68, 83
defense of Obama, 167–68
feelings about the Clintons, xi, xiv, 174, 182–84
lecturing Hillary, 110–11
recruiting Elizabeth Warren, 160
role in foreign policy, 68–69, 71, 74–75, 83, 177–78
sabotaging Hillary, xii–xiii, xv, 109–10, 174–75, 177, 184–85, 187–89, 192, 224–26, 233
Jones, Paula, 102, 200
Journal of Muslim Minority Affairs, 78
Justice Department. *See* U.S. Department of Justice

K

Kagan, Elena, 53
Kasich, John, 158
Katzenberg, Jeffrey, 54, 160
Kelly, Michael, 46
Kennedy, Bobby, Jr., 161–62
Kennedy, Caroline, 74, 162
Kennedy, Edward "Ted," 160, 162
Kennedy, Ethel, 162
Kennedy, John F., 119, 151, 182
Kennedy, Joseph, II, 161–62
Kennedy, Max, 161–62
Kennedy, Rory, 162
Kennedy Compound, 161, 163
Kennedy Curse, The, 119
Kernberg, Otto F., 40
Kerry, John, 109, 151, 177–79
Keystone XL Pipeline, 66, 160
Kissinger, Henry, 27
Kolbert, Elizabeth, 105
Kraushaar, Josh, 208

Krueger, Alan, 101
Kudlow, Larry, 99

L

Lake, Celinda, 45
Larry King Live, 52
Lasry, Marc, 98
Late Show with David Letterman, 19, 213
Latimer, Matt, 133
Lawford, Chris, 162
Lazio, Rick, 150
Letterman, David "Dave," 19, 85, 213
Lewinsky, Monica, 16, 38, 94, 109, 119, 133–34, 174, 196, 200, 213
liberals, 8, 15, 41, 49, 59, 61, 102, 109, 120, 163, 167, 183, 214, 230–31, 233–34
Libya, 86, 120–22
Lindsey, Bruce, 53, 95
Little Rock, AR, 7, 12–13, 19, 38, 91, 94–95, 121, 158, 200–1, 211
Little Saint James, 198
Living History (Clinton), 8, 39
Los Angeles Times, 5, 11, 92
Lowry, Rich, 120
"Lucy" (*Australopithecus afarensis*), 223–24
Lynch, Loretta, 189

M

Maher, Bill, 134
Mandela, Nelson, 56
Manhattan, NY, 5, 91
Margolis, Jim, 170
Maumee, OH, 212
Maxwell, Ghislaine, 97, 197–98, 200
McAuliffe, Terry, 97, 123–24

McDonough, Denis, 74
McFadden, Cynthia, 16, 213
McKinsey & Company, 95
media, the, 12, 48, 51, 59, 61, 92, 170
    coverage of Clinton Foundation, xii, 15–16, 92–93
    Hillary's and, 103, 113, 116–17, 148, 206–10
    Valerie Jarrett's leaks to, 71, 174–75, 179
Media Matters, 120
Meir, Golda, 4
Metcalfe, 113
Mezvinsky, Charlotte Clinton, 9
Mezvinsky, Edward, 97
Mezvinsky, Marc, 97–99, 219
Middle East, 67, 169, 183, 215
Mills, Cheryl, 24, 66, 121
Mitchell, George, 67
Mook, Robby, 80
Moonlite BunnyRanch, 11
Moore, Minyon, 52
Morris, Roger, 39
Mourning, Alonzo, 193
Mourning, Tracy, 193
Mourning Family Foundation, 193
Moynihan, Daniel Patrick, 48
Moynihan, Liz, 48
Mozambique, 197
Mubarak, Hosni, 86
Muskie, Edmund, 59
Muslim Brotherhood, 78
Muslim World League, 78
Myers, Dee Dee, 42, 152

N

National Action Network, 128
National Archives and Records Administration, 113

National Journal, 136, 208

National Review, 120

National Security Agency, 108

NBC News, 16, 92, 94, 99, 213, 232

Nevada, 11, 158, 218

New Hampshire, 23, 49, 57, 59–61, 150, 161, 207, 209, 213, 218, 224

New York, NY, 38, 48, 61, 72, 93, 95, 148, 150, 199, 208

New Yorker, 104–5

New York magazine, 150, 197, 230

New York Times, 54, 150, 189
  coverage of Clinton Foundation, 15, 33, 92–94, 127
  stories about Hillary, 56–57, 102–3, 109, 120, 174, 207, 209, 232
  stories about Marc Mezvinsky, 97–99

New York Times Magazine, 172–73
  stories about Hillary, 46

Nicholas, Peter, 206

Nielsen BookScan, 149

Nigeria, 12, 125–26, 197

Nightly News, 92

Nixon, Richard, 76, 116

Noah, Timothy, 59

Nobel Peace Prize, 73

Noonan, Peggy, 129

North Korea, 73, 82

O

Obama, Barack, 49, 54, 156–58, 214–15
  Africa trip, 223–24
  as amateur, 83
  foreign policy doctrine, 169
  John Kerry and, 177–78
  legacy of, 160, 184
  Oprah and, 52
  as out of the loop, 107–10
  popularity of, 16, 156, 214
  post-presidency plans, 18, 173
  refusal to help Hillary, xiii–xvi
  relationship with Clintons, xi–xiii, 14, 21, 38, 68, 72–73, 83, 168–75, 179, 181–84, 217–18, 224–26, 231, 233
  relationship with Valerie Jarrett, xi, xiii, 68, 168
  Selma and, 191–92
  Sidney Blumenthal and, 110, 120
  2008 primary, 15, 49, 52–61, 151, 160
  2012 election, 123
  whispering campaign against, 167–69

Obama, Michelle, 160, 168, 178, 187–89, 224
  feelings toward Clintons, xi, 31, 38, 68, 182–84, 224, 226, 233
  softened image, 104–5

Obama administration, 23
  investigation of Hillary's private e-mails, 220
  relationship with Hillary as secretary of state, 68, 72–76, 83

Obama White House, 122
  Hillary's meetings at, xi–xiii, 110, 182
  relationship with Hillary, 68, 71, 73–76, 82–83, 108–9, 156, 172, 174–75, 177, 179, 192, 231
  support of challengers to Hillary, 160–61, 185, 221, 233

Obeida, Najib, 120

Ohio, 158, 212

O'Malley, Martin, 25, 109, 156, 184, 233

Ornish, Dean, 31

P

Pace, Julie, 207
Paglia, Camille, 37
Palestinians, 67, 73
Palmieri, Jennifer, 170
Pardongate, 109
Partners in Power (Morris), 39
Paul, Rand, 150
Peltier, Leonard, 55–56
People, 149
Petraeus, David, 108
Pletka, Danielle, 85
Plunkitt, George Washington, 210
Podesta, John, 24, 32, 80, 142
Politico, 15, 74, 80, 92, 117, 209
President Clinton Avenue (AR), 13
Putin, Vladimir, 69, 86, 127, 143, 151, 183

Q

Qatar, 129–30

R

Reagan, Ronald, 61, 151, 174
RealClearPolitics, 96, 103, 131
Reines, Philippe, 67
Republican Party, Republicans, 49, 116, 120, 125, 134, 153, 168, 170, 181, 184, 233. *See also* GOP, the challengers to Hillary, 24, 136, 150, 157–58, 184
Rice, Susan, 178
Rice University, 206
Rich, Denise, 55
Rich, Marc, 55–56
Rieder, Rem, 117
Roberts, Andrew, 41
Roberts, Virginia, 198–200

Rock Center with Brian Williams, 92
Rock Creek Group, 99
Rodham, Dorothy Howell, 39–40, 57–58
Rodham, Hugh, Sr., 38–40
Rodham, Tony, 29, 55, 123–25
Rogers, William Pierce, 76
Roosevelt, James, III, 171
Rosatom, 127
Rose, Charlie, 147, 213
Rose, Marshall, 199
Rose Garden strategy, 205
Rose Law Firm, 38, 134, 232
Rotunda, Ronald D., 113
Rove, Karl, 14
Rubin, Robert, 173
Rubio, Marco, 136, 150, 158
Russia, 86, 127, 140–41, 143, 151, 208, 236
Rust Belt, 158
Rwanda, 197

S

Safire, William, 56
"Saint Hillary" (Kelly), 46
Sanders, Bernard "Bernie," 109, 184, 233
Sarbanes-Oxley Act, 113
Saudi Arabia, 17, 77
Scalia, Antonin, 230
Schake, Kristina, 104–5
Schoenfeld, Gabriel, 136
Schow, Ashe, 116
Schultz, Debbie Wasserman, 170, 218
Schumer, Chuck, 61, 72
Schwartz, Allan, 26–27
Schweizer, Peter, 126, 137
Scooby Doo van, 23, 209, 212
Secret Service, 13, 101, 148, 161, 209

Selma march, 191–92

Shalala, Donna, 32, 193, 219

Shameless, 219

Sharpton, Al, 128

Sheehan, Michael, 47–48

Sheinkopf, Henry, 174

Shriver, Bobby, 162

Shriver, Doug, 162

Siegal, Peggy, 199

Simon, Roger, 209

Socarides, Richard, 52

South Africa, 197

South Carolina, 14, 218

South China Sea, 86

Spacey, Kevin, 10, 197

Spence, Roy, 104

Spencer, John, 150

Spielberg, Steven, 3, 5, 43, 54, 102, 105

Stanage, Niall, 136

State Department. *See* U.S. Department of State

Steenburgen, Mary, 97

Steinberg, James, 75

Stephanopoulos, George, 199, 231

Stevens, Christopher, 122

Stewart, Mitch, 170

Stiglitz, Joseph, 101

Strassel, Kimberley A., 130

Streisand, Barbra, 160

Sullivan, Jake, 67, 121, 123

Swain, Susan, 20

T

Tanden, Neera, 53

Teneo, 79

Thatcher, Margaret "Maggie," 4

Thomas, Landon, Jr., 197

Time-Life Building, 91, 95

Travelgate, 109, 134

Trende, Sean, 103

Treuhaft, Walker and Burnstein, 102

Trumka, Dick, 157–58

Trump, Donald, 221

Trump Tower, 5

Truth about Hillary, The (Klein), 38

Tucker, Chris, 197

Tutu, Desmond, 56

20/20, 112

Twitter, 79, 209, 215, 236

2008 presidential primary
    Bill's role in, 13–14
    Hillary's losses, 57, 60–61, 71
    Iowa, 49, 51–52, 56–57, 58
    Maine, 60
    New Hampshire, 49, 57–61

2014 midterm elections, 167–68, 181–82

2016 Democratic presidential primary
    challengers to Hillary, 61, 184–85
    Hillary's advantages, 170–72
    Hillary's baggage, 61
    Obama's neutrality in, 183
    polling data, 135, 232–33
    Valerie Jarrett's role in, xiii, 175, 177, 224–26, 233

2016 presidential election
    polling data, 23–24, 135–36, 150
    Hillary's logo, 104

U

UBS, 130

Ukraine, 151, 183

Underwood, Claire, 10

Underwood, Frank, 10

UN Foundation, 125

United Arab Emirates, 17

United States, xiv, 14, 25, 95, 111, 125, 127, 130, 143, 152, 195, 230, 235

University of Arkansas Clinton School of Public Service, 12, 20, 202
University of Miami, 32–33, 193
Uranium One, 127–28
Uribe, Alvaro, 127
USA Today, 117
U.S. Department of Homeland Security, 124
U.S. Department of Justice, 108, 113, 129, 188–89, 225
U.S. Department of State, 97, 130, 151, 177–79
    Hillary's time at, 16, 38, 61, 65–68, 71–77, 79, 81, 85, 87, 91, 104, 110–16, 120–30, 134–36, 138–44, 179, 188, 232, 236
    investigation of Hillary, 175, 177, 180
    Obama White House and, 68, 71, 74–76, 175, 177–78
    Sidney Blumenthal and, xiii, 110–11, 120–21
U.S. House of Representatives, 120, 173, 236
U.S. Senate, 5, 43, 48–49, 55, 61, 66, 113, 121, 125–26, 134–36, 150, 160, 163–64, 173, 178

V

Van Natta, Don, 41
VCS Mining, 124–25
View, The, 172
Virginia, 104, 123, 158
Vitter, David, 125–26

W

Walker, Scott, 135–36, 157
Wallace, Nicolle, 172
Wall Street, 8, 17, 163, 234

Wall Street Journal, 16, 66, 130, 206, 232
Warren, Elizabeth
    Clintons' fear of, 156, 159–60
    encouraged to run by Obama White House, 160–61
    popularity among Democrats, 61, 160–61, 173, 233
    progressive politics of, 101–2, 160–61, 173, 233–35
    visit with Clintons, 163–64
    visit to Kennedy Compound, 162–63
Washington, D.C., 4, 17, 47, 85, 99, 136–37, 208, 218
Washington Examiner, 116
Washington Post, 15, 85, 103–4, 170, 189, 205–7, 214, 235–36, 240
Webb, Jim, 109, 184
Weiner, Anthony, 79–80, 97
West Wing, 21
Wexner, Leslie, 199
Whitehaven, 4, 7–8, 12, 101–2, 104, 163, 200, 218
Whitewater, 109, 134, 232
Wicks, Buffy, 170
Wilhelm, Heather, 96
Willey, Kathleen, 200
William J. Clinton Presidential Center and Park, 12
Winfrey, Oprah, 51–54, 56
Wirth, Tim, 125
Wisner, Frank, 86

Y

Yankees, 48